THE POSTAGE STAMPS
OF GREAT BRITAIN

THE POSTAGE STAMPS
OF GREAT BRITAIN

by K. M. BEAUMONT
and H. C. V. ADAMS

PART THREE
THE EMBOSSED ISSUES
THE SURFACE-PRINTED ISSUES OF
QUEEN VICTORIA AND KING EDWARD VII

LONDON
THE ROYAL PHILATELIC SOCIETY, LONDON
1954

9999045577

Preface

THE revision of Part I of the late J. B. Seymour's classic work was completed just before his death, and published in 1950. When the time came to work on Part II it was decided to devote the whole volume to the perforated Line Engraved issues, and to provide a third volume to deal with the Embossed and Surface-Printed Stamps. An Editorial Panel was formed for this purpose, and work on Part II is still proceeding.

When dealing with the surface-printed issues Seymour only went as far as 1865. The Editorial Panel agreed not only to complete the reign but to carry the story on to the end of the reign of King Edward VII. As a result this volume covers a lot of new ground, and has been written by the recognised authorities on these stamps.

Major Beaumont and Mr Adams have had the close co-operation of Mr F. C. Holland, Dr W. R. D. Wiggins and Dr H. W. Eddison, and thanks are due to them for the great care with which they have collated and verified the information available, and for having given so freely of their own research.

The illustrations in the text have been prepared from material kindly lent by Mr Adams and Major Beaumont. Furthermore each stamp has been illustrated from a plate proof, so that the details of the designs and engraving are clearer than can be seen usually from reproductions of stamps printed in fugitive inks. By gracious permission these proofs have been provided by Sir John Wilson from the Royal Collection, and the Publications Committee acknowledges his help gratefully.

A fourth volume, covering the issues of King George V, is also contemplated.

February, 1954

JOHN EASTON
ARNOLD STRANGE
Publications Committee

Contents

Illustrations

After page 180

Illustrations of the Surface-Printed Stamps of
Queen Victoria and King Edward VII
(*reproduced from plate proofs*)

Chapter One

The Embossed Adhesive Stamps

THE embossed octagonal stamps were required to meet the higher foreign postage, and also the charge for registration. Their troublesome and more costly method of production was retained until 1856, when they were replaced by other designs produced by the quicker and cheaper method of surface printing, although the One Penny and Twopence values continued to be produced by the line-engraved process to a much later date.

The adoption of these stamps was doubtless due to the fact that colour embossing presses, supplied by Dryden Bros. of Lambeth, had been installed at Somerset House since the beginning of 1841 for stamping envelopes, and also that the Mint coining-presses were available for preparing the dies.

This method served to meet the limited demand for these higher values, but the stamps were not popular, and later increasing requirements, and the convenience of perforation introduced in 1854, rendered further issues of imperforate stamps undesirable.

In the embossing process the colourless part of the design is forced up from behind by a counterpart of the die, and appears in high relief on a coloured background. The stamps were struck separately in rows on sheets, previously gummed by Perkins, Bacon & Co., which showed no spacing, and which were shifted horizontally and vertically by hand.

The designs were the work of William Wyon, who took as his model the head of Queen Victoria which had already served for the line-engraved stamps,* and he was subsequently given the task of engraving the necessary primary dies. Judging by his coloured designs for the two higher values, which are still in existence, it was originally intended that the Tenpence should be in green and the One Shilling in yellow, but this suggestion was changed before printing was undertaken. (*See* Plates I and II.)

* *The Postage Stamps of Great Britain*, Part I (revised), p. 52.

1

The head, without the pendant curl, was deeply cut in recess on an octagonal steel block, and die proofs exist with a plain background in yellow or green. From this primary die the engraving was transferred to another steel block, which was the basis of the original dies for the different values, and the supplementary engraving was done by Thomas Moss, a Government engraver, in the following manner:

First, the pendant curl was added, which differs in the three values.

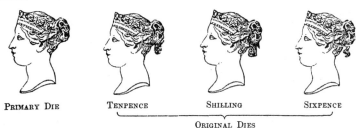

PRIMARY DIE   TENPENCE   SHILLING   SIXPENCE

ORIGINAL DIES

FIG. 1

Secondly, the white lines, and the engine-turned pattern, which differs in each value, were added, and on the Sixpence value a spray, composed of a rose, thistle and shamrock, was engraved in the lower part of the frame. The dies were then hardened, and counterparts were made in which the incised details appeared in relief and the value and POSTAGE were sunk.

All the working dies, taken from the primary dies, were eventually numbered in recess on the base of the bust together with the initials W.W.

It is evident, however, from the examination of specimen sheets and unused blocks of both the Tenpence and One Shilling values embossed by Die 1 of each, that three different varieties of them exist, namely:

(a) without Die Number or Initials;

(b) with Initials but no Die Number;

(c) with both, although sometimes hardly discernible.

It has been suggested that more than one working die was used in each case to account for this, but the generally accepted explanation is that the variations were entirely due to irregular pressure and the markings on the counterpart, or ‘ mule ’ as it is called in the trade, being insufficiently in relief to obviate this irregularity.

On Die 1 of both values the initials W.W., when they appear, precede the number, and they do so also on Die 2 of the One Shilling ; but on Die 2 of the Tenpence onwards the number precedes the initials, as it does in the case of the Sixpence issued later.

ONE SHILLING   SIXPENCE
DIE 2   DIE 1

FIG. 2

THE DICKINSON PAPER

The silk thread paper, which had been used for the Mulready envelopes of 1840 as a protection against forgery, and also experimentally tried for the line-engraved stamps at the beginning of 1841,* was made by John Dickinson & Son at their works near London. John Dickinson, the founder of the firm, had patented special machinery for the production of the silk thread paper in which the moist pulp, instead of being led over an endless wire gauze band, was picked up by a revolving gauze-covered cylinder. The silk threads were introduced as required, by supplementary rollers, while the moist pulp was still on the revolving cylinders.† The silk threads, in parallel pairs, were arranged so that a pair would run vertically through each stamp, and the mill sheet was subsequently divided into printing sheets.

The arrangements of the mill sheets and their division into printing sheets have been described by various writers, but

* *The Postage Stamps of Great Britain*, Part I (revised), pp. 10, 77, 136.
† The Dickinson machines are described in detail in *Postage Stamps in the Making*, pp. 54–56.

the following particulars are taken from two unprinted sheets, one of which was gummed, which are in the Berlin Imperial Postal Museum. While the main points of these two sheets agree, the details are taken from the gummed specimen.

The length of the sheet is 51·3 cm, and the width is 24·8 cm. The side margins of the two sheets differ, and apparently they were trimmed after the mill sheets were made. The mill sheets contain eight vertical pairs of silk threads, in two groups of four, which are divided in the centre by a threadless space.

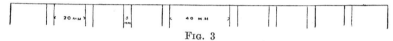

FIG. 3

In each pair the threads are approximately 5 mm apart, but there are variations on the same sheet, though the 20 mm spacing between the pairs is constant. It was evidently important that the spacing between the pairs should be regular, but otherwise exactness was not necessary. According to the authors of our standard books the mill sheets were cut into printing sheets by being divided vertically through the threadless space, and the two strips were then cut horizontally into three equal parts, giving six printing sheets of equal size. Wright and Creeke * state, and it has been accepted by all later authors, that the Berlin Imperial Postal Museum possesses an entire gummed sheet containing a silk thread running down the centre of the threadless space. This was supposed to be intended to facilitate the division of the sheet. The originator of this statement was, however, not a keen observer, as in addition to the fact that this alleged thread is simply a ruled pencil line, the sheet also shows two horizontal lines, and the spacing of these shows clearly the arrangement of the mill sheet into printing sheets of different sizes, and the reason for these variations. The upper and lower divisions measure 16·4 cm, and the centre 18·5 cm. The sheet is inscribed by hand : 'The Paper for 1s and for 10d Label stamps after gumming but before cutting.'

* *History of the Adhesive Stamps of the British Isles*, by H. B. Wright and A. B. Creeke. London : Royal Philatelic Society, 1899.

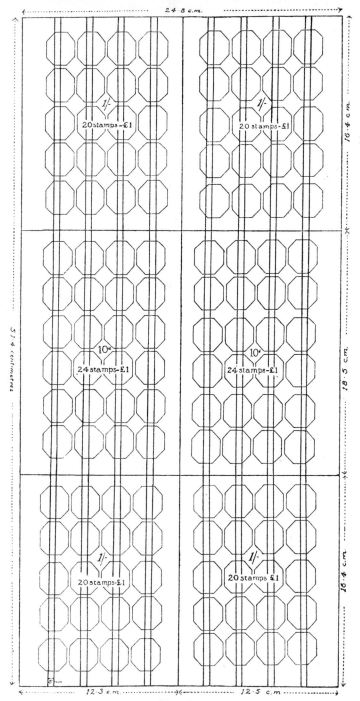

FIG. 4

The mill sheet, which is hand-stamped several times SPECIMEN, shows without doubt that the pencil lines indicate the parts to be cut into printing sheets. There can be no question that the reason for the two centre printing sheets being longer is proved by their being inscribed ' 10d ' and the upper and lower sheets ' 1s '. Further, the difference is explained by the fact that the One Shilling units required only five horizontal rows of four stamps to make up the value of one pound, while six rows were necessary of the Tenpence value. These statements lend a new meaning to the ever-recurring official designation of the silk thread paper as ' The Paper for the 1s and 10d stamps '.

Although the specimen sheet described comes from the Public Records of the Berlin Imperial Postal Museum, and shows that it was sent officially from London to the Prussian Postal Authorities for some special purpose, it might still be argued that an unprinted specimen sheet does not necessarily prove that two parts of the mill sheet were used for the One Shilling value, and only one for the Tenpence value. Such a contention cannot, however, be maintained, as the two printed SPECIMEN post office sheets of both values in the Museum show the exact measurements given. This is confirmed by the official printing warrants issued from Somerset House. These observations and deductions were made in Berlin by Munk and Seymour also inspected the sheets there in September 1930.

According to Wright and Creeke the printings from 1847 to 1853 were :—

Year	Sheets of Tenpence	Sheets of One Shilling
1847	20,000	40,000
1850	8,000	16,000
1851	16,000	32,000
1852	14,000	46,000
1853	32,000	64,000

No printing orders were issued during 1848-49.

This table shows that, except in 1852, when something unusual must have happened, exactly double the number of One Shilling sheets were printed, which confirms the present conclusions. There is an element of risk in the simultaneous printing of more than one value on the same sheet, as the numbers printed of two or more values are thus pre-determined. A similar case is that of the Finnish marginal watermarked sheets of 1895-1925.

There must have been some trouble with the printing, as that of the One Shilling value began some months earlier than the Tenpence value, but the middle of the sheet, prepared for the Tenpence value, might have been reserved in stock until required.

The question still remains as to what happened after the temporary suspension of the Tenpence value from the end of 1854 to October 1856. Either the size of the mill sheet was reduced, or the shilling sheets of 1855-56 had larger upper and lower margins than those of the earlier printings.

THE WORKING DIES

The Tenpence Value

Six working dies were prepared from the original die, but for the issued stamps only Dies 1 to 4 were used. Die 5 was employed in later years, from 1889 to 1895 inclusive, for stamping envelopes, and although copies on gummed paper have been seen at Somerset House, according to Wright and Creeke, none were ever issued. It is not known what happened to Die 6, but a Die 7 was made and used during 1896 and onwards for postal stationery.

The stamps were registered in May 1848 without a die number and, until impressions were found on whole or part sheets with and without this indication, it was assumed that all copies from initial printings did not have any number ; but as mentioned earlier this does not seem to have been the case. It also had been stated that the sheets overprinted SPECIMEN, of which some still survive, all consisted of impressions taken from the original unnumbered die, but this too has proved a fallacy, for some of

PLATE I

1   1847.   Essays for colour and design for the One Shilling
2   and Ten Pence embossed adhesive stamps.

The descriptive writing is that of Ormond Hill.

3   1847.   The original sketch for the Ten Pence embossed
stamp.   This was submitted to the authorities at the
beginning of 1847 by William Wyon, the engraver to the
Royal Mint.

The writing is that of Ormond Hill.

Shades of colour submitted for 1/-
stamp in 1847

1

Essay (of colour) submitted
for original 1o stamp in '47.

2

Original design for 1o stamp.
submitted by Wyon in 1847.

3

PLATE I

them at any rate show the same variations as the early issued sheets.

The Shilling Value

Three working dies for this value were prepared from the original die, but only Dies 1 and 2 were used for the issued stamps.

Sheets of Die 1 show the same variations as in the case of the Tenpence Die 1. Die 3 and later dies were employed for postal stationery.

The Shilling Essay

This was an experimental die which was not approved, and was therefore rejected. It shows Wyon's head, badly centred, without the pendant curl. Furthermore the engine-turned frame and the lettering differ from the approved design. Forty impressions were printed, twenty in pale yellow-green, and twenty in the red-brown colour of the Tenpence value. Of these, eleven in green and twelve in red-brown were experimentally cancelled, probably to determine the effect of the obliteration on the cameo surface. The London City No. 14 (Fig. 5) and the London District No. 67 (Fig. 6) were used for this purpose.

Fig. 5   Fig. 6

SILK THREAD VARIETIES

There are two of these. One is caused through the first impression being placed too near the margin of the sheet, resulting

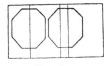

Fig. 7   Fig. 8

in only the first thread showing on the first stamp, and consequently two threads 20 mm apart on the next (Fig. 7) and following stamps, which is repeated throughout the row.

The other variety consists of stamps showing only one thread in the middle of the stamp (Fig. 8), or indifferently spaced pairs of thread, caused by the breaking or displacement of the threads in the manufacture of the paper.

From the collector's point of view, the value of these embossed stamps depends on their condition. Used examples should have clear margins and light cancellations, but as they were very closely printed, and often overlapped, perfect examples are not common. Stamps cut to shape are valueless. Unfortunately some early albums provided octagonal spaces for them which accounts for many spoilt copies. Collectors are warned against stamps with skilfully added margins, or which have been mounted.

The obliterations are usually heavy and blotchy, which is probably due to the uneven surface.

Used pairs and strips of the Tenpence and Sixpence are scarcer than in the One Shilling value. Used blocks of all three values are known, but are very rare in fine condition.

Covers with stamps up to the value of five shillings, generally with American addresses and postmarks are frequent, and those showing a combination of these stamps are interesting. The value of unused specimens depends not only on the margins, but on the perfection of the embossing, and the condition of the gum.

Unused blocks of each value exist and are of considerable rarity. Specimen stamps, generally overprinted in black, but also in red for the One Shilling value, are known, including complete sheets.

As already stated, adjoining stamps, through bad spacing, frequently show more or less overlapping, horizontally or vertically, and extreme examples are valuable, especially in pairs or blocks. Examples of partly double impressions may be found in both values. In some the embossing shows a coloured impression superimposed ; others show a slight shift in colour ; while occasionally there appears a well-separated ' ghost ' with a clear impression overlapping. Well-defined examples have fetched high prices.

Chapter Two

First Embossed Issue

TENPENCE AND ONE SHILLING VALUES 1847 and 1848

THE pendant curl and engine-turned design differ in the two values.

Coloured embossing was used and printing took place at Somerset House on Dickinson silk thread paper.

The Tenpence from Die 1 marked on base of neck WW1, or without 1, or without both WW and 1 ; and from Dies 2, 3 and 4 marked 2WW, 3WW and 4WW respectively.

The One Shilling from Dies 1 and 2 marked WW1 and WW2 or Die 1 without 1, or without both WW and 1.   Both imperforate with brownish to white gum.

Tenpence Red-brown to deep chestnut-brown : November 6, 1848
Die 1 : January 3, 1848 to March 14, 1850.
Die 2 : May 4, 1850 to December 15, 1852.
Die 3 : February 8, 1853 to December 8, 1854.
Die 4 : December 8, 1854 to April 28, 1855.
Die 5 : Not issued officially.

One Shilling Green : September 11 or 13, 1847
Die 1 : June 21, 1847 to April 28, 1855.
Die 2 : February 23, 1854 to ?

(*a*) Pale yellow-green.
(*b*) Green.
(*c*) Deep green.

Silk thread errors
(*a*) Printing error : one silk thread at each side of the stamp.
(*b*) Paper error : one silk thread through the stamp.

Both values have been found doubly embossed.

These two values form an independent issue, although there was a distance of more than a year between the dates of issue.

There is an analogy between them and the line-engraved One Penny and Twopence values of 1840, as in both cases there is a certain similarity of design, and other characteristics. It is not mere chance that the Sixpence stamp differed in design and paper, and this was due to the fact that it was a separate issue, required by later changes in postal rates.

It is therefore wrong to catalogue the three values as one issue because they were produced by embossed printing, although this is a common practice in most English, French, and German catalogues, and also in many English handbooks.

In the same way the line-engraved Three-halfpenny stamps should not be connected with the line-engraved Half-penny value as one issue from a tariff point of view, but with the One Penny and Twopence Type 3, as the Queen's head for this value also comes from Die 2 and the design is a modification of the earlier type.

According to Rowland Hill's diary the date of issue of the One Shilling stamps was September 11, 1847, although a notice in *The Times* gave the date as the 13th of that month.

The Tenpence value was put into circulation on November 6, 1848.

The ink used at first was found in course of time to wear the dies badly, owing it was stated to a grinding quality in its make-up. For that reason a new kind of ink was employed from the middle of May 1850, during the life of Die 2.

The number of One Shilling stamps issued, less waste, was 5,655,420, composed of 282,771 sheets of 20 impressions, and the last printing was made in October, 1856.

There were 2,928,000 stamps issued of the Tenpence, in 122,000 sheets of 24 impressions, and the remaining 5,085 sheets were probably destroyed as waste. The printing was discontinued at the end of 1854. At first both values were issued to the chief post offices in London, Edinburgh and Dublin, to four London branch offices, and to 109 provincial post offices. It was not until the end of April 1850, that a general issue was made throughout England, Scotland and Ireland.

The One Shilling value covered the postage to the United States of America, to many British colonies in the West Indies, to New South Wales, New Zealand, India, etc., and apparently to the British colonies in North America.

Owing to the reduction from tenpence to fourpence in the postage rates to France on January 1, 1855, the demand for Tenpence stamps so declined that they were withdrawn on August 15, 1855. At the beginning of 1862, however, there was again a demand for them, and 2,012 sheets left over at Somerset House were re-issued. These were not exhausted until late in 1866. A further demand, due possibly to a new tenpence rate to India in 1867, could not be met as the stock at Somerset House was exhausted.

Chapter Three

Second Embossed Issue

SIXPENCE VALUE : MARCH 1, 1854

THE altered frame, attributed to Ormond Hill, showed in the lower panel an embossed spray of a rose, thistle and shamrock.

Hand-made paper, manufactured by Stacey Wise, Northampton, and watermarked V R in block letters. One die, numbered IWW. Imperforate. Yellowish gum, but tinted green about the end of 1854.

Colours : Pale lilac
           Blue-lilac.
           Mauve.
           Purple.
           Violet.

Varieties : Double print.
             Embossed on gummed side.
             Watermark inverted.
             Watermark reversed.
             Watermark inverted and reversed.
             Green tinted gum.

This value was proposed in 1850, owing to the reduction in March 1848 of the registration fee from a shilling to sixpence, but the decision to issue it was not arrived at until September 8, 1851, and it was even then so delayed that the stamps were not issued until March 1, 1854.

In 1853, and the first half of 1854, the postage rate between Great Britain and the majority of the British colonies was reduced to sixpence, and a similar reduction had already been made in the rates to various European states.

The printing was begun on January 30, 1854, and continued until about the end of 1856. During this time the number of stamps printed was 6,659,920 in 166,498 sheets of 40. Although a further printing warrant was issued in October 1856, and

14

55,498 sheets were printed, no delivery for general circulation took place after September 29, 1855. It may, therefore, be assumed that the unissued 73,541 sheets (2,941,640 stamps) were officially destroyed when the first Sixpence surface printed stamps were ready for issue.

THE DIES

Four dies were registered on January 11, 1854, but only Die 1 was used for the adhesive stamps. Die 2, fitted with date plugs, was used in December 1855 for stamped envelopes, and in September 1855 Dies 3 and 4 with date plugs were also used for this purpose. In 1885 these three dies were used for stamping telegraph forms, and the sixpence telegraph rate necessitated many new dies.

The initials on the die are quite close to each other, not spaced apart with stops between, as is incorrectly stated in all English handbooks, and the figure 1 is separated from the initials by a comparatively wide space (see Fig. 2).

THE PRINTING SHEETS, WATERMARK, etc.

According to Wright and Creeke these contained forty stamps in two vertical groups of 20 (5 × 4) and were post office sheets valued at £1. They came to this conclusion because the printing warrants and account books at Somerset House showed this value as ' 40 to the sheet '. According to other views, however, which have not yet been confirmed, the post office sheets, and possibly also the printing sheets, were divided into groups of 20. The height of the sheet was about 32·4 cm and consequently the half-sheet would be 16·2 cm, and thus only very slightly less than the size of the shilling sheets of 20. But the Sixpence stamp was 1 mm longer than the One Shilling, so that the top and bottom margins of the sheet would be slightly less. In spite of this, however, reconstructed sheets prove that a mill sheet could supply two printing sheets with ample margins.

It should be noted that the normal spacing between the stamps is very slight, and that most examples show parts of the adjoining stamp.

In view of the short arms of the printing presses at Somerset House there is a possibility that both groups were printed on full sheets, but with one half-sheet inverted, as was done with the embossed fiscal stamps. This, however, cannot be verified.

The paper generally has a yellowish or creamy tone, and is usually stout ; since it was hand-made it varies in thickness.

The watermark VR appears once on each stamp. Examples with inverted watermarks are almost as numerous as the normal. It may also be found reversed, and sometimes inverted and reversed. There is no marginal watermark.

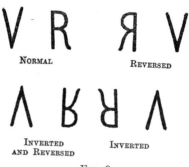

NORMAL   REVERSED

INVERTED   INVERTED
AND REVERSED

Fig. 9

As the paper was gummed before printing, the sheets showing the reversed watermark must have been gummed on the wrong side.

Pure gum arabic was used, which at first was yellowish like the paper, and owing to the clearness of the gum, sheets were sometimes printed in error on the gummed side, and inadvertently issued. In February 1855 a complaint was made to the authorities about this, and in reply Ormond Hill stated that it was difficult to distinguish the gummed side owing to the yellowish paper and to the transparency of the gum, and that in order to prevent this he had given instructions that the gum should be slightly coloured. It was, therefore, given a greenish tint.

Used examples of this error are known, but their condition is always defective.

The colour sometimes shows intense, and occasionally pale, shades. The more numerous are lilac tints, which may be found in a reddish-lilac, and a dull blue-lilac which is rather scarce.

Examples with good clear margins are scarce. Fine mint copies are expensive, while pairs and blocks are rare.

Double impressions are known.

2

Chapter Four

Surface-Printed Stamps: 1855 to 1883

In 1855 the authorities decided, with a view to economy and more rapid production, to adopt surface-printing for postage stamps, but only for the purpose of replacing the Embossed adhesive stamps, and for such new values as were found to be necessary. Production of these was entrusted to Thomas De La Rue & Co., London, who were already printing stamps for the Inland Revenue Department and who had begun to use electrotype plates about 1845.

At this time Hulot was already engaged in producing stamps from electrotypes for the French Government, and Ormond Hill went to Paris to enquire into the details of his process. Not much information was gained, as Hulot carefully guarded his working processes. It was, however, accidentally ascertained that he took lead impressions from the die, which were made up into formes, from which electrotype plates were made.

DIES AND PLATES

The original die for each design was cut in relief on steel, the design being reversed. This was transferred by pressure to lead blocks the size of the stamps. The moulds were formed in lead and not, as had sometimes been stated, in gutta percha or wax. The required number of moulds, having the design in recess, were assembled in a forme, and on them was deposited a shell of copper in an electro-chemical bath. This produced an electrotype when backed with type metal, and one or more of these were used as printing plates. Subsequently, when more extensive printings were required, master plates were employed from which any number of electros could be made. The life of these copper plates was not long until a Frenchman, Joubert,* employed as an engraver by De La Rue, patented a method in

---

* His full name was Jean Ferdinand Joubert de la Ferté.

1858 by which plates could be faced with steel and, as this could be renewed, the life of the plates was considerably prolonged, thus rendering surface-printing more practical and economical. Thereafter experiments with a nickel and chromium facing were carried out, but steel facing was employed by De La Rue throughout the printing of these issues.

In 1861 the Plates of the Four Pence value received a protecting coat of silver to prevent decomposition, which occurred through chemical action between the copper and the vermilion in the ink.

Each Plate consisted of two or more of the above-mentioned electrotypes, known as panes, which varied in number in the different values. From the beginning of 1862 the surface-printed stamps were issued with check letters in the four corners, and from 1865 the Plate Numbers were added on both sides of the stamps. Before the introduction of Plate Numbers on the stamps, in some cases distinctive Plate marks were added which enabled them to be identified.

For the insertion of the corner check letters the die was pierced to allow lettered steel plugs to be let in. The check letters and Plate Numbers first appeared in white on a coloured ground and later in colour on a white ground.

THE PAPER

The paper with Garters as watermarks for the Four Pence value, and the Emblems watermarked paper for the first Six Pence and One Shilling values, were hand-made. This was used for the Four Pence large Garter issue until June 1864, but from December 1864 machine-made paper was used. It was a wove paper manufactured by Turner & Co. of the Chafford Mills, Fordcombe, near Tunbridge Wells. The Spray and all later watermarked papers were machine-made. The watermark bits, supplied by De La Rue, were struck from sheet brass and were fastened by brass wire to the gauze in the moulds, and to the dandy rolls for machine-made paper.

The paper was normally white but, as will be noted later under the issues concerned, a bluish, or blue, or so-called safety paper, was sometimes used. Fiscal paper, which was commonly more or less tinged with blue, was also used for certain printings.

PRINTING AND GUM

According to *British Isles*,* hand presses were used until about 1880, after which steam presses were employed. The first stamp printed on the steam presses was probably the One Penny Venetian red issued in 1880. Typographic printing being a dry process, it was possible to gum the paper before printing and, as this imparted an extra hardness to the paper, it gave a sharper impression which did not penetrate the surface, and this was supposed to make the subsequent removal of obliterations more difficult. On this account, until 1856, a safety paper was used, as in the case of fiscal stamps. The gum was a clear white gum arabic which was evenly applied. It did not crack or cockle the paper, and as it was quite transparent the sheets were sometimes printed on the gummed side and occasionally issued in this condition. Sheets gummed on the wrong side caused the watermark to appear reversed. The printers gummed the sheets before sending them to Somerset House for perforation and issue to Post Offices, except in five cases mentioned hereafter.

When Wright and Creeke inspected the Imprimatur Sheets at Somerset House in 1896, they made exhaustive notes about each Sheet and incorporated the results in the Appendix of *British Isles*. The only detail which they omitted to mention was whether the Sheets were gummed or not. From the fact that many of the copies cut from the earlier Imprimatur Sheets are without gum, it was assumed by some people that it was the practice, until about 1870, for the printers to supply at least one ungummed sheet of each Plate to Somerset House for deposit in the archives for registration as an Imprimatur. But recently, through the courtesy of the Postmaster-General (the Sheets are

---

* *History of the Adhesive Stamps of the British Isles*, by H. B. Wright and A. B. Creeke.

now held by the General Post Office), it has been ascertained
that the only Imprimatur Sheets without gum are those of the
Three Pence Plate 2 (without reticulations in the spandrels), the
Four Pence Plates 1 and 2, the Six Pence Plate 1 and the One
Shilling Plate 1.   It follows therefore that, with these exceptions,
the copies in the Royal Collection and those from the Crawford
and Leonard Clark Collections, and the other copies which were
cut from the Imprimatur Sheets in 1900, originally had gum.   In
some cases the gum on the Imprimatur Sheets is very thin, and
in some cases it appears to have been partially removed.   For
the purpose of registration the printers supplied from one to
six sheets to Somerset House, and one of these was deposited in
the archives in imperforate condition as the Imprimatur impression of the Plate concerned.   What happened to the other sheets
(if any) supplied in connection with registration is described
hereafter.   In the case of the Three Pence Plate 2, Four Pence
Plates 1 and 2, Six Pence Plate 1 and One Shilling Plate 1, more
than one ungummed sheet may have been supplied, and this was
certainly so in the case of the Four Pence Plate 1.

If an imperforate stamp from one of the five Plates above
mentioned was officially gummed, it cannot have been from an Imprimatur Sheet in the archives, but, for reasons above mentioned,
it does not follow that because a stamp is ungummed, it must be
from such an Imprimatur Sheet.

In this category specimens are known with a thick brownish
gum quite unlike that used by De La Rue.   This appears on some
specimens cut from the Imprimatur Sheets, and the probable
explanation appears to be that, after a number of copies were
cut from the Imprimatur Sheets in 1900, the sheets were replaced
in books into which they were stuck with thick brownish gum.
Unfortunately this brown gum was sometimes applied to the
corners of the sheets which at that time included the remaining
Plate Numbers in the margin, which are now in the Royal
Collection.   The result is that many of the pairs in the Royal
Collection with Plate Numbers in margin, which were not cut
from the sheets until long after the original cutting in 1900,

show this brownish gum or traces of it following unskilful attempts at removal.

PERFORATION

Throughout these issues the sheets were perforated 14 at Somerset House, except for the 5 Shillings, Ten Shillings, and One Pound stamps on Maltese Cross paper which were perforated $15\frac{1}{2} \times 15$. The 14 gauge perforation combs used at Somerset House for the Garter, Emblems and Spray watermark papers, were arranged so that the gutters between the panes were perforated vertically through the centre ; but a few stamps were abnormally perforated with a single line treadle machine at Somerset House. This was used occasionally for dealing with portions of sheets which were not issued officially. These are noted later.

Except on the outer sides, the sheets included a gutter or wing margin about 5 mm wide on both sides of each pane. As these wide margins were unpopular with collectors, it was a common practice, for commercial reasons, to make the stamp symmetrical by re-perforating the side margins close to the stamps. Knowledge of the division of the sheets into two, four or twelve panes, and of the order of the check letters, enables these forged perforations to be detected. On the Three Pence, Six Pence, Nine Pence, Ten Pence and One Shilling stamps, those with wing margins on the right are lettered in the lower corners A D to T D and AH to TH, and on the left lettered A E to T E and A I to T I ; on the Four Pence and Eight Pence those with wing margins on the right are lettered in the lower corners A F to T F, and on the left A G to T G ; but this does not apply to some of the 'Abnormals', as mentioned hereafter. The Twopence Halfpenny and values above One Shilling did not have wing margins. Wing-margin copies sometimes had their perforations trimmed in order to make them appear as if they were genuine imperforate stamps. These fakes can usually be detected by measuring them vertically. If the height is less than 23 mm the probability is that they are faked wing-margin copies with the perforations trimmed.

There are, however, perfectly genuine imperforate stamps in some of the issues. Copies of these, which must not be confused with specimens cut from the sheets made for registration purposes, are known in both used and unused condition from some of the Plates. These are noted later.

PAPER CONTROLS

From July 1860 to 1881 the sheets issued to the printers were stamped with a control mark at the top of the right and at the bottom of the left margin. A different mark was provided for each value so as to ensure the correct paper being used for the required stamp. The value was expressed in figures except for the One Pound value which appeared in words.

Until 1875 the controls were stamped in blue, when the colour was changed to red. From about 1872 the position of the controls was indicated by the word 'mark' in the marginal watermark.

ESSAYS, PROOFS AND COLOUR TRIALS

(*See* Plates II to VI)

It would require a separate book to give a proper account of the work undertaken by De La Rue which led to the designs finally adopted for the various values and issues, and the changes in design of the surface printed stamps, even if all the necessary information and material were available. In fact, many of the items concerned are unique in the literal sense of that much abused expression, because only single specimens exist of some of the essays and of some of the proofs which were signed or initialled by Ormond Hill, sometimes with notes or instructions accompanied by a Treasury registration number and dated.

Judge Philbrick collected items of this character in the middle of the nineteenth century, and some of his specimens went into the Ferrary Collection, and thence to the Berlin Postal Museum, notably the only series of the earliest essays for the Four Pence, Six Pence and One Shilling values. In the early days little value

PLATE II

1 1847.   The original sketch for the One Shilling embossed stamp.   This was submitted to the authorities at the beginning of 1847 by William Wyon, the engraver to the Royal Mint.

The writing is that of Ormond Hill.

2 1856.   Die proof in bright red on glazed card of a design similar to that approved for the One Shilling value of 1856. The oval band and lettering are larger than those on the issued stamp.

The inscription is written and initialled by Ormond Hill.

3 Die proof of Nine Pence in bistre with large white letters in corners.   Die 2 similar to the issue of December 1, 1865 (Plate 4), but with figures of Plate 2.   Inscribed ' Old '.

4 Similar die proof with large coloured letters in corners, and coloured plate numbers and stars on white background.

Inscribed ' New and approved 11 March 1872—2280/72 ' in pencil in the writing of Ormond Hill.

Original design for the 1/- stamp submitted by Wyon — in 1847

1

This is the form approved by the Board 12 March 1856

But the color to be green

2

3

4

PLATE II

was placed upon such items, which are now of great philatelic interest, and many were acquired for private collections indirectly from Somerset House and De La Rue. Fortunately a number of these are now in the Royal Collection; but there are many others, some of which are in the collections of two of the Editors. Recently (1951) a number of die proofs, including proofs of essays inscribed by Ormond Hill, came upon the market upon the dispersal of the Sugden and Seymour Collections.

The issues concerned of course fall roughly into four main categories:

> Without corner letters
> With small corner letters
> With large white corner letters
> With large coloured corner letters.

Each change involved the preparation of essays and eventually die proofs of these. De La Rue were always endeavouring to lighten the design of all the stamps in order that they might show up better. Obvious instances of this principle are indicated by the removal of the so-called reticulations from the corners of the first design of the Three Pence, and the change of the design of the Six Pence with circular frame for the head to a hexagonal frame. Actually the earlier essays for the Three Pence had two lobes of the tri-lobe design at the top instead of at the bottom of the stamp, as they appear in the design eventually adopted. The artist's drawings, three in number, which led to the adoption of the three-lobed design, were acquired by one of the Editors from the Sugden Collection. These consist of sketches in Indian ink and Chinese white.

Before the first designs were chosen for the Four Pence, Six Pence and One Shilling values, a number were considered and essays and proofs of these prepared, including those now in the Berlin Postal Museum referred to above. Before the sixth issue of the Six Pence, in which the frame of the head was changed from a circle to a hexagon, essays indicate the stages which were considered before the new design was approved by Ormond Hill.

At a later stage, for the seventh and ninth issues, the positions of the Plate Number on the stamp were changed.

In connection with the change from white to coloured corner letters there are, *inter alia*, two special categories of die proofs, one marked 'Old' showing the corner letters in white, and one marked 'New' showing coloured corner letters. This applied to the Four Pence, Six Pence, Ten Pence and Two Shillings values, and in some cases die proofs were taken in twelve different colours.

There are also rare essays and die proofs in different designs and colours for the Nine Pence and One Shilling values especially, some of which bear approval notes in the writing of Ormond Hill. This applies in some cases to die proofs of designs which were not in fact adopted. Die proofs also exist in different states of the Ten Shillings and of the One Pound stamp in different designs ; and it is evident that De La Rue devoted special attention to the Five Pounds stamp, the die utilised for which was that of the Telegraph stamp of the same value.

Many of the die proofs concerned are available in black showing the die before and after hardening, and sometimes before or after striking, with the appropriate date. In some cases plate proofs also exist in black or in a variety of colours ; and colour trials from some dies and plates, the latter with or without perforation and with or without the overprint SPECIMEN.

Colour trials, other than those taken from the dies themselves (mostly not contemporaneously), were infrequent in the early days of surface printing, because the colour of the stamps was decided in advance. There is, however, a series of imperforate colour trials from Plate 15 of the Four Pence on paper with normal watermark and gum, made apparently about 1876-77 in connection with the changes in colour from vermilion to sage green and brown which were subsequently made. These were in about twelve different colours and shades. There are also imperforate colour trials of the Ten Shillings and One Pound values of the issues of September 1878. These are on normal gummed paper with watermark Maltese Cross, and overprinted SPECIMEN.

From 1880 onwards there were numerous colour trials. In

the year 1880, for some reason still unknown, more than twenty-four perforated colour trials were taken of every value then in use, with the exception of the Halfpenny and One Penny, though some were taken also of these values at another time.

On November 3, 1882, single sheets were printed from Plates 13 and 14 of the One Shilling in purple or lilac on Crown paper. These were gummed and some were perforated. Most of the latter were overprinted SPECIMEN. About the same time a set comprising the Halfpenny, One Penny, Three Half Pence, Twopence Halfpenny, Three Pence, Four Pence, Five Pence, Six Pence, and One Shilling values was prepared. This set was printed in pale lilac on normal gummed Crown watermark paper perforated 14. The Twopence Halfpenny was from Plate 23, the Three Pence from Plate 21, the Four Pence from Plate 17, the Six Pence from Plate 18 and the One Shilling from Plate 14. The other values were of the type current at the time. Each stamp was overprinted in black with a large figure and symbol of value. These were essays for a proposed unified series which was not adopted. Most of the stamps were destroyed and this set is of great rarity. It is illustrated under Nos. 97 to 106 in the Supplement to *History of the Adhesive Stamps of the British Isles.* (*See* Plate VIII.)

The Three Pence and Six Pence values had already been issued in purple overprinted with large figures and symbols of value in red.

Chapter Five

Surface-Printed Stamps : 1855 to 1883

IMPRIMATUR SHEETS AND 'ABNORMALS'

As mentioned earlier, the Imprimatur Sheets in the archives at Somerset House were printed on ungummed or gummed paper, and unused imperforate stamps cut from these sheets are well known.

Until recently considerable mystery surrounded the Imprimatur Sheets and stamps cut therefrom, and particularly concerning the extra sheets which were usually printed when each Imprimatur Sheet was struck for approval and registration, unless the plate concerned was put to press simultaneously with registration. Wright and Creeke assumed that what they describe as ' the usual five extra sheets ' were always printed at the same time as the sheet which became the Imprimatur Sheet, that is to say, that six sheets were printed, one of which was selected for the Imprimatur and placed imperforate in the archives at Somerset House. They also assumed that ' the usual five extra sheets ' were (with certain special exceptions) perforated, put into stock and issued with the stamps current at the time. Recent investigations indicate that some of these assumptions were incorrect. About 1896 Wright and Creeke inspected the Imprimatur Sheets at Somerset House and made careful notes concerning each, comprising the Plate Number, Current Number, Colour, Paper, Watermark, Date of Striking, Date Approved, Date of Putting the Plate to Press, Date of Taking from Press, Date of Defacement, Date of Destruction, Number of Impressions and Remarks. These particulars appear in the Appendix to *British Isles*.

When the Imprimatur Sheets were inspected in 1896 apparently only minor mutilations had occurred. It was not until 1900 that organised spoliation of these sheets occurred. A complete set of single copies with marginal Plate Numbers attached went into the collection of Lord Crawford. Several years later, as mentioned above, corner pairs, including the remaining Plate Numbers in the margins, were removed and placed in the Royal Collection where they still remain as part of a Royal heirloom. These two sets accounted for all the copies with marginal paper attached bearing the Plate Number, except in the case of the Four Pence Plates 1 and 2, Six Pence Plate 1 and One Shilling Plate 1, each sheet of which had four marginal Plate Numbers, but no Current Numbers. Another set (with marginal Plate Numbers of the Four Pence Plates 1 and 2, Six Pence Plate 1, and One Shilling Plate 1, and marginal Current Numbers from the Imprimatur Sheets) was acquired by the late Leonard H. Clark. In 1900 a number of other sets of single copies were cut from the sheets for officials at Somerset House or their friends. The total number cut from each sheet in 1900 was about two dozen. This involved the removal of the two top rows in the sheet. Then the pairs for the Royal Collection were removed, making twenty-six copies in all. Certain other mutilations of the Imprimatur Sheets occurred, e.g. the Nine Pence Plate 5, particulars of which are given hereafter.*

Since each copy with Plate Number attached, and each copy with Current Number attached, was in a different position on the sheet, and every copy had different corner lettering, when this was introduced with the series of 1862, it follows that each such copy from the several Imprimatur Sheets must be unique. The possibility of other sheets (from ' the usual five extra sheets ') having been left imperforate, from which copies may have been cut, is discussed hereafter. According to J. B. Seymour, the system of printing five extra sheets at the same time as the Imprimatur, and putting them into stock for issue, was not followed in the case of sheets from plates which were never put to press, although registered. These plates were the Three Pence Plate 3, Six Pence Plate 10, Eight Pence Plate 2, Nine Pence Plates 3 and 5, Ten Pence Plate 2, One Shilling Plate 3 and Two Shillings Plate 3. However, Seymour was mistaken (if he meant that *no*

---

* The number of copies removed from each Imprimatur Sheet are approximate only. The Crawford copies, and the pairs in the Royal Collection, were sometimes cut from the top of the sheet and sometimes from the bottom, and the same applies to the Leonard Clark copies with current numbers in margin.

extra sheets were printed in such cases) because used copies of all these, except the Eight Pence Plate 2, Ninepence Plate 5 and One Shilling Plate 3, are well known.

It follows from what appears above that the Imprimatur Sheets in the archives (at any rate all those subsequent to 1860) were deprived of all the marginal Plate Numbers attached, because all the copies concerned went into the Royal and Crawford Collections. It is possible, however, that in some cases similar copies from 'the usual five extra sheets' may have survived in imperforate condition. These could only be distinguished from copies from the Imprimatur Sheets if they had the same corner letters, if they differed materially in shades or if they were gummed and the Imprimatur Sheet was ungummed. In this connection it should be mentioned that many of the copies from the Imprimatur Sheets which passed into the collections above-mentioned no longer have the gum which was on all the Imprimatur Sheets, except the five referred to above.

The Crawford Collection of copies from the Imprimatur Sheets with Plate Numbers attached was acquired by Mr R. B. Sparrow in 1915 and was disposed of on his behalf by Mr Charles Nissen, from whom it was acquired in succession by Mr William Stirle and Colonel A. F. Bates. Most of these copies were subsequently acquired by one of the Editors through Mr Robson Lowe, Mr John Langham and Mr H. F. Johnson ; and one of the Editors also acquired copies from other sources, including some from the L. H. Clark Collection with marginal Current Numbers attached, and some marginal specimens from Mr Charles Nissen. Another of the Editors also acquired a number of the last-mentioned copies.

The L. H. Clark collection dispersed in 1944 contained imperforate corner marginal copies (Imprimaturs) with Plate Number attached of the Four Pence Plates 1 and 2, Six Pence Plate 1 and One Shilling Plate 1, and marginal Imprimatur copies from the other plates with Current Numbers in the margin. Consequently the Royal, Crawford, and Clark Collections would account for all the stamps with marginal Plate Numbers except four (Four Pence Plates 1 and 2, Six Pence Plate 1 and One Shilling plate 1), and all except one set with Current Numbers attached, from all the Imprimatur Sheets concerned.

It was due to the practice of making an Imprimatur printing for purposes of approval and registration, before the regular issue (when the plate was put to press), that the so-called 'Abnormals' occurred, because in these cases the Imprimatur printing was sometimes made in a colour or on paper with watermark different from that used for the regular issue, i.e. a colour or paper which was current when the Imprimatur printing was made but discontinued before the regular issue. It is difficult to explain why, in some cases, perforated 'Abnormal' used or unused copies are unknown when 'Abnormal' Imprimatur copies exist. If six sheets were printed for registration purposes, five of which were perforated and issued, one would expect to find perforated and used copies of all the stamps of which 'Abnormal' Imprimatur copies exist. Actually, however, no perforated used or unused copies are known of the Twopence Halfpenny Plates 4 and 5 with watermark Anchor, Three Pence Plate 5 watermark Emblems, Three Pence Plate 21 watermark Spray, Six Pence Plate 18 watermark Spray, Eight Pence Plate 2, One Shilling Plate 5 watermark Emblems or Five Shillings Plate 4 watermark Maltese Cross, although Imprimatur copies of all these exist.

If 'the usual five extra sheets' from each of these plates, in colours and on the papers mentioned, corresponding with the Imprimatur Sheets, were perforated and issued with the stamps having normal watermarks and similar colours for the respective issues, how does it happen that no perforated used or unused copies of any of these stamps are known ? In every case (except the Twopence Halfpenny and 5 Shillings) five sheets would represent 1,200 stamps ; in the case of the Twopence Halfpenny 1,050, and for the Five Shillings 400 stamps. It seems probable that in these cases 'the usual five extra sheets' were not printed or, if they were printed, that they were not perforated and issued. If they were printed, but not perforated or issued, what happened to them ? There is no evidence to show whether they were destroyed or survived imperforate. In the latter event it is possible that they or some of them, became available to collectors, and that copies of these exist in addition to those cut from the Imprimatur Sheets. If this is the case, there is still no evidence to show what happened to the rest of the stamps from ' the usual five extra sheets '. It seems probable that ' the usual five extra sheets ' were not printed in the case of the Twopence Halfpenny Plates 4 and 5 with watermark Anchor, Three Pence Plate 5 watermark Emblems, Three Pence Plate 21 watermark Spray, Six Pence Plate 18 watermark Spray, Eight Pence Plate 2, One Shilling Plate 5 watermark Emblems and 5 Shillings plate 4 watermark Maltese Cross, because in all these cases not a single perforated specimen, much less a used copy, is known. Perforated copies are known of the Three Pence Plate 3, Six Pence Plate 10, Nine Pence Plates 3 and 5 (unused only), Ten Pence Plate 2, One Shilling Plate 3 (unused only), and Two Shillings Plate 3.

On perforated copies of the Nine Pence Plate 5, Ten Pence Plate 2, One Shilling Plate 3 and Two Shillings Plate 3 there is no imperforate gutter margin for stamps on the outside of the panes, as in the normal stamps. That is to say, instead of the margin between the panes being perforated vertically down the middle of the marginal paper, on these stamps the perforation is close alongside the frame of the stamp, as in the case of non-marginal copies. This is easily explained in the case of the Nine Pence Plate 5 because the perforation was done specially by De La Rue on a block cut from the Imprimatur Sheet for presentation purposes. This perforation is therefore unofficial. The same phenomenon applies to a part sheet of the Three Pence Plate 3 hereafter referred to, and also to the One Shilling Plate 3. Sir Edward Bacon and Charles Nissen believed that the same phenomenon applied to the Ten Pence Plate 2 and Two Shillings Plate 3, and in fact it does apply to every known copy of these stamps (which would normally have an imperforate gutter margin) except for one single copy of the Ten Pence Plate 2 lettered H E-E H. This apparently had an imperforate gutter margin. It was in the 'A' Collection purchased by Stanley Gibbons Ltd in 1938. This would seem to prove that more than one sheet was perforated. As about thirty specimens of this stamp are known, it is possible that all 'the usual five extra sheets' were perforated and issued; but it is curious that in this case two different methods of perforation would seem to have been employed when a maximum of five sheets only was involved.

Another point to be borne in mind is that, as mentioned above, five of the earliest Imprimatur Sheets were not gummed, whereas others were gummed. This feature may have a bearing upon the mystery of some of 'the usual five extra sheets'. If six sheets were sent from the printers to Somerset House, of which one was selected as the Imprimatur for deposit in the archives, one would have expected all sheets to have been in the same state, i.e. either all gummed or all without gum. If they were all gummed then, after the Imprimatur had been selected, no difficulty would arise about having the extra five sheets perforated at Somerset House and put into stock for issue. In fact this was the normal procedure, except in connection with the five early sheets. But if the six sheets were not gummed when delivered by the printers, the extra five sheets would have had to be returned to them for gumming, and then sent back to Somerset House for perforating, before being put into stock for issue. There is no record of any such procedure. It seems, therefore, that during this early period the practice was to deliver to Somerset House only one sheet ungummed, and that further sheets (if any) delivered for registration purposes were gummed. There is at least one exception to this rule. In the case of the Four Pence Plate 1 at least two of the six sheets supplied for registration purposes were ungummed; and the same procedure may have been adopted for Plate 1 of the Six Pence and One Shilling, and perhaps also for the Three Pence Plate 2.

We know, from the copies of the Three Pence Plate 3 and Nine Pence Plate 5, which were unofficially perforated, and the mutilation of the Imprimatur Sheets, that considerable laxity prevailed at Somerset House concerning these stamps, and it

3

seems probable that, in some cases at any rate, some of the extra sheets supplied in connection with registration, or parts thereof, were destroyed or partially destroyed or left imperforate at the mercy of anyone who had access to them. For reasons given hereafter, it seems that this must have happened in certain cases which are mentioned ; and this may be the explanation if it should be found that imperforate copies indistinguishable from those from an Imprimatur Sheet exist, in addition to those from the Imprimatur Sheets themselves which were deposited in the archives. If the five extra sheets were gummed (which, as above mentioned, seems practically certain in all cases with five or six exceptions only) the survival of these would be unlikely because they would be normally perforated and put into stock for issue. For reasons mentioned hereafter, it appears evident that in some cases ' the usual five extra sheets ' were not supplied, and that only one sheet was printed, namely that registered as the Imprimatur.

Seymour stated that no strips or blocks from the Imprimatur Sheets existed, and that the only exceptions to single examples in private collections are the corner pairs in the Royal Collection. This statement is perfectly correct so far as concerns the sheets in the archives, but it does not apply to ' the usual five extra sheets ' (if any), because strips or blocks from these of the Three Pence Plate 3 are known ; one of the Editors has a strip of three of the Four Pence Plate 4, another has a pair of the Six Pence Plate 4, and there was a pair of the One Shilling Plate 3 in the Hind Sale.

When there was a substantial interval between the registration and putting to press of a plate, obviously used copies dated prior to the date of putting to press, and issue, would be from the spare sheets printed for registration purposes, and would furnish evidence that ' the usual five extra sheets ' were printed with the stamps current at the time of registration of the plate concerned.

The Nissen Imprimatur copies referred to above presumably came mainly from one or more of the sets cut from the Imprimatur

Sheets in 1900, though not apparently in the case of the copy from Plate 12 of the Six Pence. The curious feature about this copy is that it is much darker in colour than the Crawford Imprimatur copy with Plate Number in margin, and cannot possibly be from the same sheet. In this case, therefore, one (and almost certainly only one) of the six registration sheets, in addition to the Imprimatur, was left imperforate, copies from which became available to collectors. As mentioned hereafter, the registration sheets from this plate which provided ' Abnormals ', varied very considerably in colour and shade. As mentioned above, the Four Pence Plate 1 provides an instance of more than one un-gummed sheet having been supplied by the printers for registration purposes, because there is an Imprimatur copy from this plate with Plate Number in the N.W. corner margin in the Royal Collection, and one of the Editors has a similar copy from the same corner which came from the Leonard Clark Collection. Neither of these is gummed and neither shows any sign of ever having been gummed. The supply of more than one ungummed sheet for registration purposes would seem to have been abnormal, but it may have occurred also in connection with Plate 1 of the Six Pence and Plate 1 of the One Shilling, all of these representing the first issue of surface-printed stamps, and all being on deeply-blued paper. It is possible that it also occurred with the Three Pence Plate 2.

In considering these issues, it must be remembered that the Small Anchor and Orb paper for the Twopenny Halfpenny had 192 stamps in two panes of 96 each ; the Garter paper (Small, Medium, and Large) had 240 stamps in four panes of 60 each ; the Emblems and Spray papers had 240 stamps in twelve panes of 20 each ; the Large Crown paper had 240 stamps in two panes of 120 each ; the Maltese Cross paper had 80 stamps in four panes of 20 each ; and the Large Anchor paper had 56 stamps in one pane.

The following is a summary of the conclusions which can justifiably be reached concerning the Imprimatur Sheets and ' the usual five extra sheets ' (if any) of the stamps concerned, excepting the ' Abnormals ' which are dealt with later :

(a) *When the Plate was put to press for bulk printing at or about the same time as the Imprimatur Sheet was struck for approval*, it is probable that all sheets (other than the one set aside imperforate for the archives) would be perforated, put into stock and issued. There would be no point in selecting for special treatment five sheets (in addition to the Imprimatur) from a large number delivered at the same time by the printers. Therefore it seems reasonable to conclude that, *in this category*, no sheets were left imperforate at registration except the Imprimatur. Consequently the only imperforate unused specimens which exist would be those cut from the Imprimatur Sheets, apart from copies which are known to have come from a sheet which accidentally escaped perforation. These exist only in the case of a few plates, and authentic copies are nearly always used.

(b) It is not possible to be so confident about the *position when there was a considerable interval between the date of registration and the date of putting the plate to press.* In these cases if ' the usual five extra sheets ' were struck off at the same time as the sheet selected for the Imprimatur, and if the extra sheets were immediately perforated, put into stock and issued, with the sheets from plates then current, one would expect to find used copies from these sheets dated prior to the date of the plate being put to press. As will be apparent, from particulars given hereafter, there are numerous cases in which many months, and even years elapsed between the date of registration and the date of putting the plate to press. Yet no copies from sheets in this category have been recorded. At least four explanations are possible. Either ' the usual five extra sheets ' were not printed, or they were printed and left imperforate, or they were destroyed, or they were printed and perforated but not issued until bulk printings from the plate concerned were made. There is no evidence for or against the first possible explanation except such as can sometimes be deduced from the paper warrants, and the fact that Wright and Creeke refer to the printing of five extra sheets as ' usual '. Assuming that such five extra sheets were printed, what happened to them ? The absence of dated copies leads one to suppose that they were not issued at once. It seems unlikely that they would be left lying about (imperforate or perforated) for months, if not years, until the plate concerned was put to press simply because they had a Plate Number later than those of plates already at press. If they were left imperforate, one would expect either that they would still be preserved or that they would have been cut up for officials and friends before the Imprimatur Sheets were cut into. But we know that all the Imprimatur Sheets were cut, and we cannot prove that imperforate copies resembling those cut from the Imprimatur Sheets exist, unless it can be established that there are such copies having the same corner letters as stamps still on, or known to have been cut from, the Imprimatur Sheets. It has never been suggested that such sheets have been preserved imperforate, and none such are known. Therefore it seems necessary to conclude either that, *in this category*, extra sheets were not printed for registration purposes or that they were destroyed after the Imprimatur Sheet had been selected. The former alternative seems more probable ; and if *either* of these deductions is correct, we must conclude that, in this category, apart from sheets accidentally left imperforate and issued thus, no imperforate unused copies exist except those cut from the Imprimatur Sheets.

Information concerning the Imprimatur Sheets, ' the usual five extra sheets ' and the ' Abnormals ' is included under the particulars of each plate.

The following is a list of the ' Abnormals ' which were perforated, with approximate numbers of recorded copies :

Three Pence Plate 3 (Secret Dot). Officially perforated used copies from one, or more probably two, sheets, and two unused copies ; also unofficially perforated unused copies (perhaps only one pane of twenty stamps).

Four Pence Plate 16. Vermilion. Four recorded copies, all used.

Four Pence Plate 17. Green. A very few recorded copies, all used.

Six Pence Plate 10. Five recorded copies, all used.

Six Pence Plate 12. Chestnut. Several used copies in various shades of chestnut.

Six Pence Plate 13. Buff. About eighteen recorded copies, all used.

Nine Pence Plate 3. Three unused and about twenty-seven used copies recorded.

Nine Pence Plate 5. From twelve to twenty ungummed unused copies, cut from the Imprimatur Sheet, specially perforated by De La Rue.

Ten Pence Plate 2. About thirty used copies, and one unused recorded.

One Shilling Plate 3. Three unused copies perforated un-officially.

One Shilling Plate 14. Green on Spray paper. Four used copies recorded.

Two Shillings Plate 3. A very few used copies, and one unused, recorded.

The following 'Abnormals' also exist as imperforate Imprimatur specimens, but they are unknown (and almost certainly never existed) perforated, either by the official comb machine or even by the line treadle machine which was occasionally used unofficially at Somerset House for perforating a portion of a sheet :

> Two Pence Halfpenny Plates 4 and 5 Wmk Anchor ;
> Three Pence Plate 5 Wmk Emblems ;
> Three Pence Plate 21 Wmk Spray ;
> Six Pence Plate 18 Wmk Spray ;
> Eight Pence Plate 2 Wmk Garter ;
> One Shilling Plate 5 Wmk Emblems ;
> 5 Shillings Plate 4 Wmk Maltese Cross.

In most, if not all, of these cases the probability is that only one sheet (the Imprimatur impression in the archives) was printed ; in which case each of the copies cut therefrom must be unique, because each had different corner lettering.

Chapter Six

Surface-Printed Stamps : 1855 to 1883

STANLEY GIBBONS'S Catalogue (Nos 62 to 163) divides these issues into the following categories :

1855-57 *No letters in corners*
Four Pence. Wmk Small, Medium and Large Garter.
Six Pence Wmk Emblems.
One Shilling. Wmk Emblems.

1862 *Small uncoloured corner letters with Wmk large Garter for Four Pence, and Wmk Emblems for other values*
Three Pence Plates 2 and 3, Four Pence Plates 3 and 4, Six Pence Plates 3 and 4, Nine Pence Plates 2 and 3, One Shilling Plates 2 and 3.

1865-67 *Large uncoloured corner letters : Watermarks as before*
Three Pence Plate 3, Four Pence Plates 7 to 14, Six Pence Plates 5 and 6, Nine Pence Plates 4 and 5, Ten Pence (Error Wmk Emblems), One Shilling Plate 4.

1867-80 *Wmk Spray of Rose*
Three Pence Plates 4 to 10, Six Pence Plates 8 to 10, Nine Pence Plate 4, Ten Pence Plates 1 and 2, One Shilling Plates 4 to 7, Two Shillings Plates 1 and 3.

1872-73 *Large uncoloured letters in corners : Wmk Spray*
Six Pence Plates 11 and 12.

1867-83 *Wmk Maltese Cross or Anchor*
5 Shillings, Ten Shillings, One Pound and Five Pounds.

1873-80 *Large coloured letters in corners*
Twopence Halfpenny Plates 1 to 20 (*Wmk Anchor or Orb*), Three Pence Plates 11, 12 and 14 to 20 (*Wmk Spray*), Six Pence Plates 13 to 17 (*Wmk Spray*), One Shilling Plates 8 to 14 (*Wmk Spray*), Four Pence Vermilion, sage-green and brown Plates 15 to 17 and Eight Pence Plate 1 (*Wmk Large Garter*).

1880-83   *Wmk Imperial Crown*
> Twopence Halfpenny Plates 21 to 23, Three Pence Plates 20
>   and 21, Four Pence Plates 17 and 18, Six Pence Plates
>   17 and 18 and One Shilling Plates 13 and 14.

For the purposes of this book, however, it seems better to follow the method adopted by Wright and Creeke in *British Isles*, and to treat each value in sequence through the various issues and plates.

TWO PENCE HALFPENNY

First Issue: July 1, 1875

Plate 1

Registered, with Current No. 465, in lilac-rose on Anchor Wmk paper, and put to press on March 30, 1875. The plate consisted of 192 stamps in two panes of 96 stamps each, vertically disposed in eight horizontal rows of twelve. The large coloured corner lettering ran from AA-AA to LP-PL. The Plate Number appears on both sides of each stamp. The Plate Number in circle appears in the margin above the eleventh stamp in the top row of the upper pane, and below the second stamp in the bottom row of the lower pane. The Current Number appears above the second stamp in the top row of the upper pane, and below the eleventh stamp in the bottom row of the lower pane. The colour chosen was officially described as 'maroon', but is usually known as 'rosy-mauve' or 'lilac-rose'. Copies on paper more or less deeply blued are not uncommon. As the plate was put to press on the day it was registered, presumably all the sheets, except the Imprimatur, were perforated and issued, though the possibility that one or more sheets were left imperforate cannot be excluded. However, no copies of any such sheet have been recorded or identified. Wright and Creeke describe the paper of the Imprimatur Sheets of Plates 1 to 5 as 'white (fiscal) faintly blued chemically'. The blueing is so faint that it might pass unnoticed unless comparison is made with copies on really white paper.

Plate 2

Registered March 30, 1875, with Current No. 466, on Anchor paper. Put to press June 18, 1875. There is an error in the last stamp in the eighth horizontal row of the upper pane of this plate, which is lettered LII-FL instead of LH-HL ; otherwise the remarks concerning Plate 1 apply. Copies from this Plate, including unused specimens, on more or less blued paper, are known which are certainly genuine, though it is not difficult to apply a bluish tint to a stamp on normal white paper. Authentic copies of this variety are rare. Although there was an interval of two and a half months between registration and putting to press, there is no record of any sheet, other than the Imprimatur, remaining imperforate. Therefore remarks similar to those made in connection with Plate 1 would seem to apply also in this case to the Imprimatur Sheet and the lack of any other imperforate sheet.

Plate 3

Registered June 10, 1875, with Current No. 473, on Anchor paper. Put to press June 12, 1875. 20,000 sheets were printed on Anchor paper. Perforated used copies on deeply blued paper, including a copy on entire in the collection of one of the Editors, are known. Although the authenticity of this variety has been doubted until recently, the copies concerned are evidently genuine and have been certified as such by the Expert Committee. They are very rare. The paper warrants give no indication that ' the usual five extra sheets ' were supplied in connection with the registration of this Plate ; and as it was put to press two days after registration, one would assume that no sheet, other than the Imprimatur, was left imperforate. As above mentioned, however, one cannot exclude the possibility that another sheet may have been left imperforate, copies from which may have become available to collectors, though no such specimens have been identified. The blueing of the Imprimatur Sheet in this case is almost imperceptible.

Second Issue: May 31, 1876

Plate 3 also yielded 15,000 sheets on Orb paper, the make-up of which was the same as before.

Plate 4

Registered July 13, 1875, with Current No. 474, on Anchor paper. Not at press on Anchor paper. Put to press on Orb paper April 21, 1876, more than nine months after registration on Anchor paper, and issued May 31, 1876. No perforated copy on Anchor paper, either unused or used, is known. It is practically certain that none such ever existed, and that the only copies on Anchor paper are imperforate specimens from the Imprimatur Sheet itself. The paper warrants indicate that ' the usual five extra sheets ' were not printed in this case. Except as mentioned above, remarks similar to those concerning Plate 1 apply.

Plate 5

Registered July 13, 1875 (the same date as the registration of Plate 4), with Current No. 475, on Anchor paper. Not at press on Anchor paper. Put to press on Orb paper July 3, 1876, nearly twelve months after registration on Anchor paper. It should be noted that the Current Numbers of Plates 3, 4 and 5 are consecutive. No perforated copy on Anchor paper is known, either used or unused, and it is practically certain that none such ever existed. The paper warrants indicate that in this case ' the usual five extra sheets ' were not printed, and that in consequence the only copies on Anchor paper would be imperforate specimens from the Imprimatur Sheet.

Plate 6

Registered March 3, 1876, with Current No. 501, on Orb paper. Put to press September 7, 1876. If ' the usual five extra sheets ' were printed at the time of registration, and if they were perforated, put into stock and issued, copies therefrom would be indistinguishable from those of the regular issue. *British Isles* does not refer to extra sheets being printed at registration in connection with any of the Plates from 6 to 17 inclusive. The question would be of interest only if it should prove that one or more of the extra sheets were left imperforate and survived destruction. In that event, duplicates of copies from the Imprimatur Sheets would be possible. But none have been recorded. If a used copy is found dated prior to the date of putting to press, it would almost certainly be from one of ' the usual five extra sheets ', and prove that these, or one or more of them, were perforated and issued. But none such are known. The marginal positions of the Plate Number and Current Number are the same as for Plate 1.

Plate 7

Registered September 11, 1876. Current No. 513. Put to press February 16, 1877.

Plate 8

Registered April 5, 1877. Current No. 531. Put to press June 4, 1877.

Plate 9

Registered July 11, 1877. Current No. 535. Put to press September 14, 1877.

Plate 10

Registered September 20, 1877. Current No. 543. Put to press December 7, 1877.

Plate 11

Registered December 13, 1877. Current No. 547. Put to press March 19, 1878.

Plate 12

Registered April 30, 1878. Current No. 555. Put to press July 25, 1878.

Plate 13

Registered August 22, 1878. Current No. 565. Put to press September 30, 1878.

Plate 14

Registered November 15, 1878. Current No. 568. Put to press February 11, 1879.

Plate 15

Registered March 19, 1879. Current No. 575. Put to press May 8, 1879. Imperforate colour trials in blue from this plate are known, presumably made in anticipation of the change of colour which occurred in February 1880.

Plate 16

Registered June 26, 1879. Current No. 576. Put to press August 15, 1879.

Plate 17

Registered (in lilac-rose) September 19, 1879. Current No. 581. Put to press December 23, 1879. Probably only 5,000 sheets in lilac-rose were printed from this plate.

Third Issue: February 5, 1880

The remaining 30,000 sheets from this plate were printed in blue.

Plate 18

Registered (in blue) January 22, 1880. Current No. 583. Put to press February 11, 1880.

Plate 19

Registered and put to press April 6, 1880. Current No. 588.

Plate 20

Registered May 28, 1880. Current No. 592. Put to press October 11, 1880.

Fourth Issue: March 23, 1881

Plate 21

Registered and put to press on paper with Wmk Crown February 3, 1881. Current No. 625. Each sheet comprised 240 stamps in two panes vertically disposed. Each pane of 120 stamps is described as a ' Post Office ' Sheet. It had corner lettering from A A-A A to L T-T L.

On sheets with the Crown watermark no Plate Number or Current Number appears in the margin.

Plate 22

Registered June 11, 1881. Current No. 626. Put to press June 9, 1881. In this case the plate was put to press two days before registration. The Current Numbers of Plates 21, 22, and 23 are consecutive.

Plate 23

Registered June 11, 1881. Current No. 627. Put to press June 9, 1881. In this case also the plate was put to press two days before registration. Plate 23 is recorded imperforate ; but an (unused) imperforate copy would be indistinguishable from one cut from the Imprimatur Sheet unless there was a marked difference in shade or the corner letters were the same.

Obviously when a plate was put to press at or about the same time as the Imprimatur Sheet was registered, there would be no point in printing ' the usual five extra sheets ' with the Imprimatur copy, because there would be hundreds of sheets from which to select the latter. This confirms the theory that the extra five sheets, often referred to by Wright and Creeke, were frequently mythical rather than usual. All sheets printed by De La Rue went imperforate to Somerset House, where the perforation was effected ; and De La Rue had to account for every watermarked sheet issued to them, including spoiled sheets.

Chapter Seven

Surface-Printed Stamps : 1855 to 1883

THREE PENCE

FOR the First Issue the plate was composed of 240 stamps in twelve panes of 20 stamps arranged in four horizontal rows of three panes each. Each pane of 20 stamps in five horizontal rows of four constituted a Post Office sheet. The Plate Number appeared only twice in the full sheet of 240 stamps, namely, in the margin above the third stamp in the top row of the N.E. corner pane and below the second stamp in the bottom row of the S.W. corner pane. The Current Number appeared above the second stamp in the top row of the N.W. corner pane and below the third stamp in the bottom row of the S.E. corner pane. The corner letters ran from A A-A A to L T-T L, as if the sheet consisted of a single pane of 240 stamps. The paper until 1867 was watermarked Heraldic Emblems. There is an error of watermark showing three roses and a shamrock, instead of two roses a shamrock and a thistle, on stamp AT-TA from Plates 2 and 4, and presumably also from Plate 3. As this error does not appear in all the Imprimatur Sheets concerned it is evident that more than one dandy-roll was used.

Plate 1

This was defective and never registered.

First Issue : May 1, 1862

Plate 2

Registered (in the original condition with reticulations in spandrels) October 17, 1861, with Current No. 208, in carmine on Emblems paper, and put to press the following day. 1,500 sheets were printed from the plate in this condition, but none of these were issued. Imperforate and perforated copies are well known, both with and without SPECIMEN overprint. Perforated copies without the overprint are rare. Indeed, Lord Crawford

had the following note in his collection concerning the original
state of Plate 2 : ' Copies are known perforated without the
overprint " Specimen ". The only one I have ever seen is a well-
executed forgery.' After removal of the reticulations from the
spandrels, the plate was re-registered in carmine, and put to
press on March 19, 1862. The first supplies were received by the
General Post Office on the 26th and 28th of April 1862. The
date of issue was May 1. In this case again there would be no
question of ' the usual five extra sheets ' being specially printed
with the Imprimatur impression, because the plate was at press
from the moment the Imprimatur Sheet was registered ; and
British Isles in this case refers to ' a single sheet for the Imprimatur
of the altered plate '. But imperforate Imprimatur copies from the
altered plate exist in more than one shade. Therefore one or more
of the extra registration sheets must have been left imperforate.
The Imprimatur Sheet of Plate 2, as re-registered, is one of the
five or six without gum. The Imprimatur Sheet as originally
registered is gummed.

Plate 3

(' Secret Dot.') Registered August 25, 1862, with Current
No. 218, in carmine on Emblems paper. The so-called ' Secret
Dot ' consists of a small white dot inserted on each side of the
stamps just below the foliate ornament. This plate was never
put to press, but ' the usual five extra sheets ' were evidently
printed. A very few used copies with official perforation (and two
unused copies) are known. These are much darker in shade than
the Imprimatur Sheet. As they differ in shade and registration
of perforation, it would appear that at least two (probably no
more) of ' the usual five extra sheets ' were officially perforated
and put into circulation. Two at least of the used copies came
from Yarmouth. A part of another sheet (perhaps only one pane)
was unofficially perforated by the treadle line machine at Somerset
House. These stamps lack the gutter margins which appear on
the stamps with official perforation ; they were found in the desk
of an official at Somerset House. Imperforate copies in different

shades are also known from two (or three) more of ' the usual five extra sheets ', including an imperforate strip of three with Plate Number in margin and a block of four (from the ' Baronet ' Collection), a pane of twenty with Current Number in margin (from the ' Avery ' Collection) and a marginal corner pair in the collection of one of the Editors.   Also about twenty-six copies were cut from the Imprimatur Sheet itself, of which a pair with Plate Number in margin is in the Royal Collection.   The marginal positions of the Plate Number and Current Number are the same as in Plate 2.

Second Issue : March 1, 1865
Plate 4

This plate with large white corner letters and Plate Number in white on either side of stamp, was registered on November 28, 1864, with Current No. 237, in carmine-pink on Emblems paper. Put to press December 19, 1864.   Most of the sheets from this plate were on Emblems paper.   If ' the usual five extra sheets ' were printed at registration, and perforated and issued, they would be indistinguishable from the regular issue on Emblems paper. No imperforate used copies are known ; and it is probable that all the imperforate copies which exist consist of those (about twenty-six) cut from the Imprimatur Sheet itself, though one cannot exclude the possibility that one or more of ' the usual five extra sheets ' were retained imperforate and that copies were cut from these.   There is, however, no evidence of this.   The marginal positions of the Plate Number and Current Number are the same as in Plate 2.

Third Issue : July 1867

The rest of the printings from Plate 4 (11,005 sheets) were on Spray paper for the Third Issue.   The make-up of the sheets is the same as for the Emblems paper.

Plate 5

Registered October, 1865, with Current No. 254, in carmine-pink on *Emblems* paper.   Put to press (on *Spray* paper only)

December 18, 1867, twenty-six months after registration on the Emblems paper. No perforated or used copy on Emblems paper is known, and the available evidence appears to indicate that the only copies on this paper which exist are those imperforate specimens cut from the Imprimatur Sheet itself. Imperforate copies from Plate 5 with Spray watermark have been recorded. These obviously could not be from the Imprimatur Sheet which was on Emblems paper. Imperforate gutter margin copies should be studied carefully, because many of these had perforations clipped. The marginal positions of the Plate Number and Current Number are the same as before. Unused imperforate copies of Plate 5 on very deeply blued Spray paper exist. These form part of experiments made by Dr Perkins with the approval of the Authorities. Perforated copies on much less blued paper, overprinted SPECIMEN, also exist. None such were issued for use.

Plate 6

Registered June 8, 1868, with Current No. 307, on Spray paper. Put to press June 22, 1869. Otherwise as before. Imperforate copies have been recorded. If unused they would be indistinguishable from Imprimatur copies unless the corner letters are similar.

Plate 7

Registered February 20, 1869, with Current No. 328. Put to press October 19, 1871. Otherwise as before.

Plate 8

Registered February 22, 1872, with Current No. 376. Put to press February 29, 1872. Otherwise as before. Imperforate copies have been recorded. If unused they would be indistinguishable from Imprimatur copies unless the corner letters are similar.

Plate 9

Registered April 22, 1872, with Current No. 382, in deep carmine-pink. Put to press July 31, 1872. Otherwise as before.

4

Plate 10

Registered December 6, 1872, with Current No. 407, in pale carmine-rose. Put to press January 1, 1873. Otherwise as before. Imperforate copies have been recorded. If unused they would be indistinguishable from Imprimatur copies unless the corner letters are similar.

Fourth Issue : July 1873

Plate 11

With large coloured, instead of white, check letters in the corners of each stamp ; registered December 21, 1872, with Current No. 414, in carmine-rose. Put to press April 17, 1873. Otherwise as before.

Plate 12

Registered June 21, 1873, with Current No. 424, in bright carmine-rose. Put to press September 4, 1873. Otherwise as before.

Plate 13

This was defective and not registered or put to press.

Plate 14

Registered August 27, 1873, with Current No. 433, in carmine-rose. Put to press January 12, 1874. Otherwise as before.

Plate 15

Registered November 25, 1873, with Current No. 435, in carmine-pink. Put to press June 9, 1874. Otherwise as before.

Plate 16

Registered June 10, 1874, with Current No. 447, in carmine-rose. Put to press October 29, 1874. Otherwise as before.

Plate 17

Registered September 30, 1874, with Current No. 455. Put to press February 20, 1875. Otherwise as before.

Plate 18

Registered January 26, 1875, with Current No. 459, in bright carmine-rose. Put to press July 13, 1875. Otherwise as before.

Plate 19

Registered May 7, 1875, with Current No. 468. Put to press March 8, 1876. Otherwise as before.

Plate 20

Registered and put to press November 29, 1878, on Spray paper (as before), with Current No. 570, in carmine-rose.

Fifth Issue : January 1, 1881

Re-registered on paper with watermark Large Crown on February 19, 1881. Copies cut from both Imprimatur Sheets, i.e. the one on Spray paper and the one on Crown paper, are known. The marginal position of the Plate Number and Current Number on the Spray paper are the same as before. The Crown paper had no Plate Number or Current Number in the margin.

Plate 21

Registered July 15, 1880, with Current No. 594, in carmine-rose *on Spray paper*. It was not put to press on Spray paper ; and was re-registered on Crown paper on July 18, 1881. No perforated or used copy on Spray paper is known, and such evidence as there is indicates that only one such sheet (the Imprimatur in the archives) was printed. Copies from both Imprimatur Sheets, i.e. the one on Spray paper and the one on Crown paper are known. The corner lettering and the marginal positions of the Plate Number and Current Number on the Spray paper are the same as before. The Crown paper had no Plate Number or Current Number in the margin.

Sixth Issue : January 1, 1883

On November 23, 1882, the Plate was re-registered in purple (with overprint ' 3d ' in red), without change of Current Number, on Crown paper. The date of putting to press in the changed colour is not recorded. There are two settings of the overprint— one has the underlying dots $1\frac{1}{2}$ mm from the ' d ' of ' 3d '. In the other the distance is 2 mm.

Chapter Eight

Surface-Printed Stamps : 1855 to 1883

FOUR PENCE

Plate 1

Registered July 13, 1855, without Current Number, on thick highly-glazed paper chemically blued all over, with watermark Small Garter. Put to press apparently on July 13, 1855. The plate, comprising 240 stamps, was divided into four panes, two and two, each consisting of 60 stamps in ten horizontal rows of six. The Plate Number appeared in concentric circles at each of the four corners of the sheet. As above-mentioned, it seems that in this case at least two ungummed sheets (including the Imprimatur) were supplied to Somerset House in connection with registration. The printings from this plate can be divided into the following categories :

First Issue

Watermark Small Garter
July 31, 1855 to October 1856
Thick highly-glazed paper

(*a*) Paper deeply blued ; shades varying from very pale to deep bright carmine. *Variety*, Double perforation.

(*b*) Paper slightly blued ; shades similar to (*a*).

(*c*) Paper nearly white ; pale to deep carmine.

(*d*) Paper quite white ; bright carmine. This variety can only be distinguished from the issues of November 1856 and January 1857 if dated prior to November 1856.

November 1856 and January 1857
Thick highly-glazed white paper

Shades of dull and bright carmine. These issues were made after those on Medium Garter paper of February, August and

November 1856, presumably from a stock of Small Garter glazed paper in which no prussiate of potash was incorporated.

Second Issue

Watermark Medium Garter
February 1856

(a) *Thick highly-glazed paper, normally more or less deeply blued.* Shades of very pale to very deep carmine.

(b) *Highly-glazed white paper.* Carmine shades. These stamps are on quite white paper and differ entirely from those of the pale rose-carmine issue on the ordinary white paper of November 1856.

August/September 1856. Two thousand sheets in very pale carmine on *ordinary thin white paper*. These stamps differ entirely as to paper, ink and colour from the regular issues of February and November 1856. They are referred to on page 94 of *British Isles*. They sometimes have the watermark inverted.

Third Issue

November 1, 1856. Ordinary white wove paper with specially prepared ink described as dull rose. Shades of pink to bright rose, quite different from the pale carmine of August 1856.

Although the later issues (August and November 1856) on white paper with Medium Garter were supposed to include varieties on thick glazed and azure papers, it is not possible to substantiate that genuine copies of such ever existed. No marked variation in the thickness of the paper of these issues can be detected ; and in view of the intensive investigation of these stamps by Wright and Creeke it must be concluded that stamps of the final issues with watermark Medium Garter never genuinely existed on azure paper, although stamps of the succeeding issue with watermark Large Garter (January 1857) are known on what might be called thick glazed paper. Ordinary white paper can be blued without difficulty.

Fourth Issue

Watermark Large Garter
January 1857
Ordinary White Paper

Wright and Creeke give the colour of the Imprimatur Sheet as ' dull and pale to deep rose, and pink '. Stanley Gibbons describes it as rose-carmine or rose. Copies are known on thick glazed paper ; but Wright and Creeke give reasons for doubting the authenticity of specimens on azure paper. It is easy to apply blueing to the paper of this issue, especially when the stamp is not an original cover. No satisfactory copy of this variety is known to the Editors.

Plate 2

Registered October 29, 1855, without Current Number, on thick highly-glazed Small Garter deeply blued paper. Forty-five sheets only were printed on Small Garter paper, and none with Medium Garter. Copies cannot be distinguished from Plate 1 unless the Plate Number on the marginal paper in the corner is attached. No such copies are known except imperforate specimens cut from the Imprimatur Sheet, the paper of which is more deeply blued than that of Plate 1. Presumably all the forty-five sheets (except the Imprimatur) from Plate 2 on Small Garter paper were perforated and issued with supplies from Plate 1. Plate 2 was put to press on Large Garter paper on June 7, 1857, as part of the Fourth Issue.

Fifth Issue : January 15, 1862

Plate 3

Registered November 29, 1861, with Current No. 206, in carmine-vermilion on Large Garter paper ; and put to press the following day. There are small white corner letters running from A A-A A to L T-T L. The Plate Number appeared in the margin above the penultimate stamp in the top row and below the second stamp in the bottom row. The Current Number appeared above the second stamp in the top row and below the penultimate stamp in the bottom row. No question arises concerning extra sheets for registration purposes because regular printing for issue began almost simultaneously with registration ; but it is possible that at least one sheet, in addition to the Imprimatur, was left imperforate, from which copies were cut.

Plate 4

Registered June 27, 1862, with Current No. 216, in vermilion-red on Large Garter paper. Put to press September 7, 1873. This plate was similar in all respects to Plate 3, except that in the latter there is a small Roman number ' I ' beside the S.W. corner square. On Plate 4 the numeral is ' II ' and there are ' hair lines ' across the corner squares. Otherwise the state of Plate 4 is the same as Plate 3. Plate 4 is recorded imperforate unused. Such copies may, however, be from the Imprimatur Sheet. They would not be distinguishable therefrom unless there is a marked variation in shade or the corner lettering is the same as that of a copy from the Imprimatur Sheet. One of the Editors has a strip of 3 from this Plate imperforate unused. This may be from one of the extra sheets printed at registration which remained imperforate. No strips from any Imprimatur sheet are known. When copies were cut from these, the only pairs were those now in the Royal Collection. All the other copies removed were single specimens.

Plates 5 and 6

These were not registered or put to press.

Sixth Issue : July, 1865

Plate 7

Registered June 3, 1865, with Current No. 247, in deep orange-vermilion on Large Garter paper. Put to press June 5, 1865. This and the succeeding Plates up to 14 had large white corner letters and the Plate Number on each side of the stamps. The colour was shades of vermilion. The Imprimatur Sheets of Plates 7 to 14 inclusive have the watermark upright. On the issued stamps, Plates 7, 13, and 14 have the watermark upright ; Plates 10 and 11 have the watermark inverted; most of the stamps from Plate 8 have the watermark upright ; and Plates 9 and 12 have about half the watermarks upright and half inverted. The marginal positions of the Plate Number and Current Number are the same as for Plate 3. For Plates 7 to 14 inclusive, if six sheets were printed for registration purposes and five of these were perforated, put into stock and issued, there would be nothing to distinguish them from the regular issue unless the position of the watermark differed from that of the Imprimatur Sheet, or there is a marked difference in shade, or the corner letters are the same. Here again, and indeed throughout these issues (except where otherwise mentioned), one cannot exclude the possibility of one or more of ' the usual five extra sheets ' having remained imperforate, from which copies were cut.

Plate 8

Registered August 15, 1865, with Current No. 248, in dark vermilion. Put to press January 23, 1866. Otherwise as before.

Plate 9

Registered November 2, 1866, with current No. 275. Put to press May 16, 1867. Otherwise as before.

Plate 10

Registered December 22, 1866, with Current No. 276. Put to press March 17, 1867. Otherwise as before.

Plate 11

Registered September 10, 1868, with Current No. 315, in orange-vermilion. The date of putting to press is not recorded, but this was apparently at the end of 1868. Imperforate unused copies from this plate have been recorded ; but these may have been from the Imprimatur Sheet. Otherwise as before.

Plate 12

Registered November 28, 1868, with Current No. 321. Put to press March 21, 1870. Imperforate unused copies from this plate are also recorded ; but these may have been from the Imprimatur Sheet. Otherwise as before. Imperforate copies on blued paper are known. Presumably these formed part of the experiments made by Dr Perkins, which are referred to under Plate 5 of the 3d. They were not issued.

Plate 13

Registered January 1, 1869, with Current No. 322, in deep orange-vermilion. Put to press October 11, 1872, more than forty-five months after registration. Any copy from this plate dated prior to October 11, 1872, would obviously be from one of ' the usual five extra sheets ' ; but none such has been recorded. Otherwise as before.

Plate 14

Registered April 1, 1869, with Current No. 327, in vermilion-red. Put to press May 8, 1873, over four years after registration. No copy is known dated prior to putting to press. See remarks concerning Plate 13. Otherwise as before.

Seventh Issue : March 1, 1876

Plate 15

Large coloured corner letters. Registered in vermilion June 10, 1874, with Current No. 428. Put to press November 17, 1875. Probably 15,000 sheets printed in vermilion. Otherwise as before.

Eighth Issue : February 27, 1877

This plate was re-registered in green on November 1, 1876, and another Imprimatur Sheet placed in the archives marked ' Impression taken as a specimen of change of colour '. The marginal positions of the Plate Number and Current Number are the same as before. A number of colour trials were made from this plate. Plate 15 in green is known imperforate unused (including a pair), and a used pair has been recorded ; but these were probably colour trials.

Plate 16

Registered in *Vermilion* August 4, 1874, with Current No. 449. Put to press in *Green* October 23, 1877. Four perforated used copies in vermilion have been recorded, but no unused

PLATE III

1   Proof in bistre from the ' Old ' die prepared in 1872 for the Four Pence.
    It is inscribed by Ormond Hill.

2   Proof in vermilion of the ' New ' die with corner letters and plate number in colour on white ground.
    This proof is inscribed by Ormond Hill ' Approved 11 March 1872—2280/72 '.

22 February 1872

4d.

Pulled in wrong color by
mistake H.H.

1

2

PLATE III

perforated specimen. From the alignment of the perforation of the recorded copies, it would seem that two at any rate of ' the usual five extra sheets ' were perforated and issued. Imperforate copies, other than those cut from the Imprimatur Sheet, are unknown ; but it is possible that one or more of the spare registration sheets remained imperforate from which copies were cut. The state of the plate was the same as before.

Ninth Issue : July, 1880

Plate 17

Registered in *Green* July 30, 1877, with Current No. 540. Put to press in *Brown* June 10, 1880. A very few perforated used copies in Green are known, but no such copy unused. The only known dated copy is dated September 17, 1877, and all the recorded specimens seem to have been used in Bradford. The alignment of the perforations indicates that at least two sheets were perforated. Wright and Creeke refer to ' the usual five extra sheets ' having been printed in green and issued, but one cannot exclude the possibility that one or more of the spare sheets were left imperforate from which copies were cut. The marginal positions of the Plate Number and Current Number are the same as before. The regular issue in Brown on Garter paper was small.

Tenth Issue : January 1, 1881

The bulk of the printings from Plate 17 were on the Crown paper.

Plate 18

Registered in Brown and put to press August 15, 1882, with Current No. 688, on paper with watermark Crown. The Plate Number and Current Number do not appear in the margins of the Crown paper. This consisted of two panes, one above the other, each comprising 120 stamps in ten horizontal rows of twelve. The corner lettering of the stamps was the same as before.

Chapter Nine

Surface-Printed Stamps : 1855 to 1883

SIX PENCE

First Issue : October 21, 1856

Plate 1

Registered and put to press March 29, 1856, on deeply-blued paper watermarked with Heraldic Emblems. No Current Number. The colour was deep violet ; but the issued stamps were generally in shades of lilac or mauve. They had no corner letters, and the Plate Number does not appear on the stamps ; but it appears in the margins at each of the four corners of the sheet, which consisted of 240 stamps arranged in twelve panes, in four horizontal rows of three, each pane containing 20 stamps in five horizontal rows of four. Two panes constituted a Post Office Sheet of 40 stamps. The Imprimatur impression is upon stout, highly-glazed and deeply-blued paper. As usual, about twenty-six copies were cut from this, including the corner copies with Plate Number in margin. Perforated copies of the regular issue on thick highly-glazed blued paper exist ; also copies on normal thin paper which is more or less deeply blued. Some such specimens are undoubtedly genuine and have been so certified by the Expert Committee. A number of experiments with blueing by means of prussiate of potash were made about this time, and it is evident that some sheets of normal thin paper were treated in this way before printing. As it is not difficult to fake such blueing, copies on blued or azure paper, especially when these are not tied to original covers, or pieces thereof, should be carefully studied or expertised before they are accepted as genuine specimens of this variety. As the plate was registered and put to press simultaneously, and as the Imprimatur Sheet is on highly-glazed deeply-blued paper, it is probable that a number of issued sheets were also printed on this paper ; but Wright and Creeke state that ' the greater part of the first printing was evidently on the thinner white paper of the later consignments '. This differs completely from the highly-glazed deeply-blued paper. Imperforate used copies on the white paper have been recorded. These would obviously be from a sheet accidentally left imperforate. Some of the colour trials were impressed with special cancellations.

Plate 2

This was not registered or put to press.

Second Issue : December 1, 1862

Plate 3

This had small uncoloured corner letters running from A A-A A to T L-L T, but no Plate Number on the stamps. Registered October 17, 1861, with Current No. 207, in lilac on Emblems paper. Put to press September 9, 1862. The Plate Number appears in the margin above the penultimate stamp in the top row and below the second stamp in the bottom row. The Current Number appears above the second stamp in the top row and below the penultimate stamp in the bottom row. Imperforate copies were cut from the Imprimatur Sheet as usual, and it is practically certain that at least one of ' the usual five extra sheets ' printed for registration purposes was left imperforate, from which copies were cut. If the rest, or any, of the extra sheets were perforated and issued, they would be indistinguishable from the regular issue unless dated prior to September 9, 1862. None such are known. Copies are known on thick highly-glazed paper. The existence of genuine copies on azure paper is doubtful.

Plate 4

This is distinguished by ' Hair Lines ' across the corner squares, and was registered in deep lilac on April 15, 1862, with Current No. 212. Put to press April 11, 1864. Otherwise as before. As unused imperforate copies (including a pair) exist, which are gummed and clearly not from the Imprimatur Sheet, it is probable that ' the usual five extra sheets ' were printed and that at least one of these was left imperforate, from which copies were cut. Specimens from any such sheets as were perforated and issued would be indistinguishable from the regular issue unless dated prior to April 11, 1864. None such are known. A copy on thick (highly glazed) paper was recorded recently.

Third Issue : April 1, 1865

Plate 5

This had large white corner letters and the Plate Number in small circles on each side of the stamps. Registered December 30, 1864, with Current No. 238, in purple on Emblems paper. Put to press January 4, 1865. The marginal positions of the Plate Number and Current Number are as before. Copies from this plate, and from Plate 6, lettered A T-T A have the watermark variety showing three roses and a shamrock with no thistle. Specimens exist from Plate 5 on extra thick paper with the watermark almost invisible.

Plate 6

Registered December 5, 1865, with Current No. 253, in purple on Emblems paper. Put to press November 22, 1866, and 12,000 sheets were printed on Emblems paper.

Fourth Issue : June 1867

This plate was then used for printing 60,000 sheets on paper with watermark Spray of Rose. The marginal positions of the Plate Number and Current Number are the same as before. In the middle of 1868 the colour was changed from dull lilac to purple, violet or bright lilac. Stanley Gibbons records specimens from this plate which were doubly printed.

Plate 7

This was not registered or put to press.

Fifth Issue : March, 1869

Plate 8

The design was altered by omitting the hyphen between SIX and PENCE. Registered January 23, 1868, with Current

No. 301, in lilac on Spray paper. Put to press December 18, 1868. Imperforate copies are known, both unused and used. Probably the lack of perforation of one or more sheets was accidental in the course of normal issue. This appears to be more likely than that one or more of 'the usual five extra sheets' (if any) printed for registration purposes should have been issued without being perforated. Unused imperforate copies could only be distinguished from copies cut from the Imprimatur Sheet by a difference in shade or similarity of the corner letters. Wright and Creeke describe the colour of the Imprimatur Sheet as lilac. Stanley Gibbons describe the issued stamps as mauve. The marginal positions of the Plate Number and Current Number are the same as before, the Plate Number being in colour within a circle.

Plate 9

Registered February 20, 1869, with Current No. 329, in deep lilac on Spray paper. Put to press May 3, 1870. Imperforate copies, both unused and used, are known also from this plate. Remarks thereon similar to those under Plate 8 apply. Wright and Creeke describe the colour of the Imprimatur Sheet as deep lilac. Stanley Gibbons describe the issued stamps as mauve. The marginal positions of the Plate Number and Current Number are the same as before. Experimental printings from this plate were made on deeply-blued paper varying in shade ; but stamps from such printings were not issued.

Plate 10

Registered April 1, 1869, with Current No. 331, in bright lilac-purple on Spray paper. Never put to press. The paper warrant shows that only one sheet of paper was ordered specially for this plate. But it is evident that more than one sheet was printed because, apart from the Imprimatur in the archives (from which copies were cut, as usual), perforated used copies are known, though no unused perforated copy has been recorded. If, as seems probable, all the known imperforate copies were cut from the Imprimatur Sheet, it is reasonable to suppose that 'the usual five extra sheets ' were printed for registration purposes and that these (or one or more of them, not exceeding five) were perforated, put into stock and issued with sheets from Plates 8 and 9. If so, the extra five sheets would seem to have been taken from a requisition for twenty-four sheets made about the time of the registration of this plate. But there is no definite evidence to show how many sheets (not exceeding five) were perforated and issued. Only five perforated specimens, all used, have been recorded, of which two were used from London, one from Weymouth and one from Aberystwyth. This number is so small that perhaps only one sheet was perforated and issued. The marginal positions of the Plate Number and Current Number are the same as before.

Sixth Issue : April 1, 1872
Plate 11

With changed design, but still with large white corner letters and the Plate Number on both sides of the stamps towards the bottom. Registered January 5, 1872, with Current No. 375 on Spray paper. Put to press January 25, 1872. Two interesting somewhat similar proofs exist showing that the new design was built up from a die proof of the previous design. One of these is in the Royal Collection. The other came into the possession of one of the Editors from the Sugden Collection. It is inscribed by Ormond Hill. Wright and Creeke describe the Imprimatur Sheet as ' dark chestnut-brown with a tinge of bronze in it, quite different from the colour of the stamps as issued '. The colour of the issue ranged from very dark to light chestnut. The marginal positions of the Plate Number and Current Number were the same as before. 20,000 sheets were printed from this plate in varying shades of chestnut. On this plate the stamps with corner letters NE and NF (at the bottom) show the figure '11' on the left partly double or distorted.

Seventh Issue : October, 1872

Then 15,000 sheets were printed in buff, the issue of which began in November 1872.

Plate 12

Registered April 22, 1872, with Current No. 381 on Spray paper. Put to press October 30, 1872. The Imprimatur Sheet is in what Wright and Creeke describe as ' light chestnut-brown '. The Seventh Issue, the printing of which began on October 30, 1872, was in buff. ' The usual five extra sheets ' were printed with the Imprimatur, and these would all seem to have been in *varying* shades of chestnut, because unused imperforate copies and used perforated copies which differ in shade from the Imprimatur Sheet and from each other exist. In this case it seems that the printers may have deliberately printed the six sheets required for registration in different shades, so that the authorities at Somerset House could make a choice, which seems also to have occurred in the case of the Three Pence Plate 3. About six copies in ' light chestnut-brown ' (really a cold greyish-brown, differing materially from the Imprimatur Sheet) from Newcastle-on-Tyne have been recognised as ' Abnormals ' from this plate ever since 1897. These range in date from August 1872 to March 1873. More recently copies in quite deep chestnut, bearing no resemblance to buff, have been recorded from Halifax, Manchester, London, Liverpool, Cheltenham and Suez, ranging in date up to January 1874. It is certain that, in addition to the Imprimatur, one at least of the six sheets concerned was left imperforate because of the difference in colour between the Crawford and Nissen imperforate copies from the registration sheets, which have already been mentioned. Of the remaining four sheets, one was perforated and presumably went to Newcastle-on-Tyne. It seems probable that the remaining three of ' the usual five extra sheets ' were also perforated, and that portions thereof went to Halifax, London, Liverpool, Manchester and Suez, from which a pair on entire is known which appears to be in one of the chestnut shades. No unused perforated copy in chestnut is known. The very wide range of dates of recorded specimens, in various shades of chestnut, from Plate 12 (from August 1872 to January 1874) is extraordinary. When this plate was put to press on October 30, 1872, the colour was

5

changed to buff. Only 5,000 sheets were printed thus. Imperforate used copies in buff have been recorded but any such should be carefully studied because of the practice of trimming the perforations from wing-margin copies already referred to. The marginal positions of the Plate Number and Current Number were the same as before. On this Plate the stamps with corner letters DE and DF (at the bottom) show the figure ' 12 ' on the left partially double or distorted.

Eighth Issue : April, 1873

As from April 1873 Plate 12 was used for printing the Eighth Issue in greenish-grey until October 10, 1873, and 30,000 sheets were printed in this colour. Yet copies of the ' Abnormals ' in chestnut are known dated not only after the issue in buff but even after the printings in grey had ceased.

Plate 13

This plate had large *coloured* corner letters, and the positions of the Plate Number on the stamps were altered to the middle of the sides. Registered in *buff* December 21, 1872, with Current No. 413, on Spray paper. Put to press in *grey* December 11, 1873. ' The usual five extra sheets ' were printed in buff for registration purposes, and some, if not all, of these were perforated and issued, because used copies are known, though no unused perforated specimen. Most of the recorded copies (about eighteen in number) were used at Leeds, and single specimens have been recorded from Liverpool, Manchester and Queenstown. Wright and Creeke treat this ' Abnormal ' as a variety of the Seventh Issue because it is printed in buff, although it has the coloured corner letters which distinguish the Ninth Issue. Imperforate copies in buff cut from the Imprimatur Sheet exist, as usual. The marginal positions of the Plate Number and Current Number were the same as before. Copies in grey are recorded imperforate.

Ninth Issue : April 1, 1874

For the Ninth Issue 34,995 sheets from Plate 13 were printed in grey. The state of the plate was of course unaltered.

Plate 14

This plate, with large coloured corner letters, was registered on Spray paper. Put to press October 16, 1874. On Plates 14 to 17 the marginal positions of the Plate Number and Current Number were the same as before, until the introduction of the Crown paper which had no Plate Number or Current Number in the margin.

Plate 15

Registered July 15, 1874, with Current No. 442, in grey on Spray paper. Put to press November 26, 1875. Otherwise as before.

Plate 16

Registered September 10, 1875, with Current No. 488, in grey on Spray paper. Put to press November 2, 1877. Otherwise as before. Imperforate copies have been recorded, but these may be those cut, as usual, from the Imprimatur Sheet.

Plate 17

Registered December 13, 1877, with Current No. 546, in greenish-grey on Spray paper. Put to press April 21, 1880. Probably 15,000 sheets printed on Spray paper.

Tenth Issue : January 1, 1881

Re-registered on Large Crown paper on February 25, 1881. This paper comprised 240 stamps in two panes of 120 stamps, in ten horizontal rows of twelve, one above the other, with no Plate Number or Current Number in the margin. Otherwise as before.

Plate 18

Registered July 15, 1880, with Current No. 593, in grey on *Spray* paper. Put to press on *Large Crown* paper on January 11, 1881. No perforated unused or used copy of Plate 18 on Spray paper has been recorded. Probably only one sheet (the Imprimatur) was printed on this paper, though it is just possible that 'the usual five extra sheets' were printed. But no copy from any such has been identified. Imperforate copies cut from the Imprimatur Sheet exist, as usual. Otherwise as before.

Eleventh Issue : January 1, 1883

This Plate was re-registered on November 23, 1882, in purple overprinted ' 6d ' in red.   On stamp IO-OI the two dots, or the left-hand dot, under the ' d ' of the overprint are missing.   These omissions occur on all the sheets, including the Imprimatur. On stamp J S-S J the dots are slanting.   The space between the ' d ' and the dots is either $1\frac{1}{4}$ or $1\frac{1}{2}$, according to the setting of the overprint.

Chapter Ten

Surface-Printed Stamps : 1855 to 1883

EIGHT PENCE

Only Issue : September 11, 1876

Plate 1

Registered in purple-brown on July 7, 1876, with Current
No. 503, on Large Garter paper. The plate comprised 240
stamps, in four panes, arranged two and two of 60 stamps each,
in ten horizontal rows of six. The Plate Number appeared in
the margin above the last stamp in the top row and below the
first stamp in the bottom row. The Current Number appeared
above the first stamp in the top row and below the last stamp in
the bottom row. The date of putting to press is not recorded,
but Wright and Creeke assumed that it was prior to July 31, 1876.
10,000 sheets were printed in purple-brown. Nearly all of these
were destroyed, but imperforate and perforated copies exist in
unused condition only. The regular issue was in orange. Since
the plate was not re-registered in orange, all copies from the
Imprimatur Sheet are in purple-brown. Imperforate colour
trials in three different shades varying from brown-orange to
yellow-buff, on paper with normal watermark and gum, exist
overprinted ' Specimen '. The corner lettering of the stamps
runs from A A-A A to L T-T L.

Plate 2

Registered in orange on September 11, 1876, with Current
No. 510, on Large Garter paper. It was never put to press.
Wright and Creeke state that ' the usual five extra sheets '
were printed and presumed that these were issued. There is
no evidence to support this presumption, and no unused or used
perforated copy of this stamp is known. If ' the usual five extra
sheets ' were printed, it is possible that they, or some of them or
parts thereof, survived imperforate from which copies were cut,

in addition to those cut from the Imprimatur Sheet. Imperforate copies are not of extreme rarity, and it is possible that not all of those which exist were cut from the Imprimatur Sheet itself. The marginal positions of the Plate Number and Current Number were the same as for Plate 1.

Chapter Eleven

Surface-Printed Stamps: 1855 to 1883

NINE PENCE

First Issue : January 15, 1862

Plate 1

Was not registered or put to press.

Plate 2

Registered and put to press November 14, 1861, with Current No. 205, in ochre-brown on Emblems paper. Issued specimens are in bistre and straw. The plate consisted of 240 stamps in twelve panes arranged in four horizontal rows of three, each pane containing 20 stamps in five horizontal rows of four. The small white corner letters extend from A A-A A to L T-T L. The Plate Number appears in the margin above the penultimate stamp in the top row and below the second stamp in the bottom row of the whole sheet; and the Current Number above the second stamp in the top row and below the penultimate stamp in the bottom row. There is no record of 'the usual five extra sheets' having been printed. As the plate was put to press simultaneously with registration, there would be nothing to distinguish stamps from any such sheets from those of the regular issue. The usual copies were cut from the Imprimatur Sheet. Used copies have been recorded on azure paper, but the genuine existence of this variety is doubtful, although experiments with blued paper were being made about this time.

Plate 3

This plate had 'Hair Lines' across the corner squares. Registered May 8, 1862, with Current No. 214, in bright bistre on Emblems paper; but never put to press. Wright and Creeke refer to the existence of both imperforate and perforated specimens. At least twenty-seven perforated copies have been recorded, used from at least nine different places in England. One of the Editors has a mint copy and two other unused

71

specimens have been recorded. Since not more than five sheets could have been perforated, it is evident that only part sheets can have been issued to some, if not all, of the Post Offices concerned. The imperforate copies referred to by Wright and Creeke may have been cut from the Imprimatur Sheet itself. As this is one of the least rare of the ' Abnormals ', and its use has been recorded from so many different places, the probability is that most (and probably all) of ' the usual five extra sheets ' were perforated and issued, in which case imperforate specimens must be from the Imprimatur Sheet, unless a sheet was accidentally issued imperforate, of which there is no record.   Apart from the ' Hair Lines ' across the corner squares, the state of this plate was the same as Plate 1.   These ' Hair Lines ' are sometimes faked on copies from Plate I.

Second Issue : December 2, 1865

Plate 4

This plate had large white corner letters and the Plate Number on both sides of each stamp. Registered February 27, 1865, with Current No. 239, in straw on Emblems paper. Put to press May 24, 1865, but only 3,005 sheets were printed on Emblems paper. The stamp lettered AT-TA has the error of watermark showing three roses and shamrock with no thistle.

Third Issue : October, 1867

The rest of the printings from Plate 4 (23,500 sheets) were on Spray paper. The marginal positions of the Plate Number and Current Number were the same as before. Probably all the imperforate copies with Emblems watermark which exist were cut from the Imprimatur Sheet. Imperforate copies with Spray watermark have been recorded. These must have been from a sheet which was accidentally issued imperforate, because the Imprimatur printing was on Emblems paper.

Plate 5

Registered April 24, 1866, with Current No. 255, in straw on Emblems paper ; but never put to press. Unused perforated copies exist. These are all from a part of the Imprimatur Sheet which was perforated by De La Rue early in 1887 for insertion in twelve souvenir albums for presentation to members of the Stamp Committee. About three dozen copies were cut from the Imprimatur Sheet for this purpose; but after allowing for twelve to twenty copies for the souvenir albums, the remainder (all perforated) were returned to the archives. Wright and Creeke record a used specimen discovered shortly before the publication of their work in 1899. This might have been one of the copies from the Imprimatur Sheet perforated by De La Rue, which was passed through the post not earlier than 1887, because there is no record of any of these stamps having been officially perforated at Somerset House. The fact that De La Rue resorted to the Imprimatur Sheet for specimens required for the souvenir albums indicates that no imperforate sheet, other than the Imprimatur, existed in 1887. All the available evidence points to the conclusion either that the Imprimatur Sheet was the only one printed from this plate, or that any extra sheets printed in connection with registration were destroyed before 1887. Wright and Creeke record the destruction of 230,660 of the Nine Pence Stamps in December 1876, and the waste or spoilage of 83,860. If ' the usual five extra sheets ' ever existed (and the paper warrants indicate that they may have) perhaps the 1,200 stamps concerned were included among those destroyed in 1876. It is possible, however, that imperforate copies cut from ' the usual five extra sheets ' (if such were printed) exist. This could only be decided by comparing their corner letters and shade with known copies from the Imprimatur Sheet. None such have been recorded. The marginal positions of the Plate Number and Current Number were the same as before.

In December 1872 a new die for the Nine Pence was prepared, and die proofs of this exist in black and various colours ; but it was never used.

Chapter Twelve

Surface-Printed Stamps: 1855 to 1883

TEN PENCE

Only Issue : July 1, 1867

Plate 1

Registered and put to press March 22, 1867, with Current No. 286, in red-brown on Spray paper. Large white corner letters and Plate Number on both sides of the stamps. The plate consisted of 240 stamps in twelve panes in four horizontal rows of three, each containing 20 stamps in five horizontal rows of four. The corner letters ran from A A-A A to L T-T L. The Plate Number appeared in the margin above the penultimate stamp in the top row of the sheet and below the second stamp in the bottom row. The Current Number appeared above the second stamp in the top row and below the penultimate stamp in the bottom row. On the stamps lettered AA the figure ' 1 ' of the Plate Number is smaller than that on the other stamps. Wright and Creeke record imperforate copies, but these may have been cut from the Imprimatur Sheet. Owing to a printers' error, one or more sheets were printed on Emblems paper. Only ten copies of this rare error have been recorded, seven of which were used in Constantinople and one in London. No unused copy is known.

Plate 2

Registered August 30, 1867, with Current No. 293, in pale red-brown on Spray paper ; but never put to press. In this case it is probable that most, if not all, of ' the usual five extra sheets ' were perforated and issued. About thirty used specimens have been recorded, and Wright and Creeke mention an unused copy. This presumably is the one lettered G R-R G, formerly in the Crawford Collection and now in the Royal Collection. It is not quite certain that this copy is unused. It has marks which indicate that the cancellation may have been removed. A used pair, including a wing-margin copy lettered D P-P D, has been recorded. This shows the vertical perforation along the side of the stamp instead of down the middle of the gutter margin between the panes, as would have been the case in a sheet from Plate 1. A single with wing margin possessed by one of the Editors is perforated similarly. This indicates that the spare sheets (or at any rate one of them) printed in connection with the registration of Plate 2 were not perforated by the normal comb machine at Somerset House and it is probable that all the sheets of this ' Abnormal ' (not exceeding five) were perforated vertically alongside the stamps, leaving no imperforate ' gutter ' margin. The above mentioned specimen is the only recorded case of an ' Abnormal ' in a used pair, unless a pair, already mentioned, on entire from Suez of the Six Pence Plate 12 is authenticated as being in a chestnut shade of the Imprimatur printing. Many of the specimens come from the correspondence of Messrs Crosse & Blackwell to India. The unused imperforate copies which exist were probably all cut from the Imprimatur Sheet, from which twenty-four copies, lettered A K to A L, R E to R F, S E to S I and T A to T I, were cut, in addition to the pair in the Royal Collection. The marginal positions of the Plate Number and Current Number were the same as in Plate 1. In December 1872 a new die for the Ten Pence was prepared. This was not used, but die proofs exist.

PLATE IV

1 Die Proofs of Essays of the Ten Pence taken in 1872 prior
2 to the general change over from uncoloured to coloured
   letters in the four corners of the design.   Neither of these
   was adopted.

3 Die proof of an essay for the Six Pence value of 1873.

4 Proof of the ' Old ' die with large white corner letters, which
   was adopted for the issue of April 1872.

5 Die proof of the ' New ' die which was not adopted when
   the coloured corner letters were first introduced for Plate 13,
   in November 1872.
   This proof is inscribed on the front by Ormond Hill ' Approved 11 March, 1872—2280/72 ' and on the reverse
   ' Proofs in various tints and shades to be arranged upon a
   sheet or sheets for future reference, 1 March 73.   O.H.'

6 Die proof of the Two Shillings struck in 1872 to show the
   effect of coloured letters on white corners, and plate numbers
   in central position.

7 Die proof of the Four Pence Die 3, after the corner squares
   had been altered from black to white to take coloured
   instead of uncoloured letters.

1

2

3

4

5

6

7

PLATE IV

Chapter Thirteen

Surface-Printed Stamps: 1855 to 1883

ONE SHILLING

First Issue : November 1, 1856

Plate 1

Registered June 27, 1856, with no Current Number, in bright green on stout, highly-glazed, deeply-blued Emblems paper. Put to press October 12, 1856. A trial printing on the thick blued safety paper was rejected, but used copies on this paper are known. Copies are also known on normal thin paper which is more or less blued. These are in the same category as similar stamps in the first issue of the Six Pence, and appear to be the results of various experiments which were being made about this time with a view to incorporating prussiate of potash in the paper, for the purpose of lessening the risk of ink and other cancellations being removed. As it is not difficult to give a bluish tinge to the paper of these stamps, especially when removed from their covers, specimens on so-called azure paper should be carefully scrutinised or expertised. Proofs in the normal colour exist on white paper without watermark. The plate contained 240 stamps in twelve panes arranged in four horizontal rows of three, each pane comprising 20 stamps in five rows of four. The Plate Number in a circle appears in the margin at each of the four corners of the sheet. Imperforate copies cut from the Imprimatur Sheet exist, as usual, and it is possible that there are similar copies from 'the usual five extra sheets'; but there is no record of any such.

Second Issue : December 1, 1862

Plate 2

(Numbered ' 1 ' on the stamps.) This was registered on May 8, 1862, with Current No. 213, in pale green on normal white paper with Emblems watermark. Put to press October 8, 1862.

The stamps had small white corner letters running from A A-A A to L T-T L.   The Plate Number appeared in the margin above the penultimate stamp in the top row and below the second stamp in the bottom row of the sheet.   The Current Number was above the second stamp in the top row and below the penultimate stamp in the bottom row.   The stamp lettered D K-K D had the ' K in circle ' variety, caused by the ' K ' plug not having been driven quite home into the die before this was pressed into the lead mould.   This variety is not shown on the Imprimatur Sheet. Otherwise the make-up of the sheet was the same as Plate 1 ; and similar remarks apply concerning imperforate copies cut from the Imprimatur Sheet.

Plate 3

(Numbered ' 2 ' on the stamps.)   This was registered on June 16, 1862, with Current No. 215, in bright green on white Emblems paper.   It was not put to press.   Only one sheet of paper was provided for the registration of this plate ; but ' the usual five extra sheets ' (or some of them) must have been printed because imperforate, and a few perforated, copies are known which did not come from the Imprimatur Sheet itself.   No used perforated copy is known, and it would seem that none of the stamps from this plate were perforated officially.   It appears that one pane of twenty stamps was unofficially perforated by the treadle line machine at Somerset House, as in the case of the Three Pence Plate 3.   Only three perforated unused copies have been recorded, lettered respectively C B-B C, A T-T A and D A-A D.   The perforation was along the vertical frames of the stamps, and not in the middle of the gutter margin, which goes to confirm that the unofficial treadle line machine was used.   At least one of the extra sheets printed for registration purposes was left imperforate (though possibly one pane of this was perforated as mentioned above), because imperforate copies, in addition to those cut from the Imprimatur Sheet, are known, including two pairs.   It seems probable that ' the usual five extra sheets ' were printed, but left imperforate (except for the pane of twenty referred to above), and that specimens from some or one of these became available to collectors. The marginal positions of the Plate Number and Current Number were the same as for Plate 2.

Third Issue : February, 1867

Plate 4

This plate, with large white corner letters, was registered on November 28, 1864, with Current No. 236, in green on Emblems paper. Put to press December 8, 1864. 39,011 sheets were printed thus. One of the Editors has an imperforate used copy of this, which does not seem to have been previously recorded.

Fourth Issue : August, 1867

The paper was then changed to Spray watermark, of which 77,000 sheets were printed from Plate 4. The marginal positions of the Plate Number were the same as before. The stamp lettered A T-T A on Emblems paper shows the error of watermark with three roses and a shamrock without the thistle. Imperforate used copies on Spray paper from this plate have been recorded ; and stamps (imperforate unused only) from this plate on Spray paper which is deeply blued are known. These represent experiments made by Dr Perkins with a view to preventing the possibility of removing cancellations. Used copies are also known in light blue (instead of green). These are probably faked changelings.

Plate 5

Registered March 28, 1866, with Current No. 256, on *Emblems* paper. Not put to press until February 20, 1871, and then only on *Spray* paper. No perforated unused or used copy on Emblems paper is known. No imperforate copies, other than those cut from the Imprimatur Sheet, have been recorded. Wright and Creeke mention that ' the usual five extra sheets ' were *presumably* printed on Emblems paper but give no evidence in support of this presumption. No copy from any such sheet seems to have survived, and it appears either that the extra sheets were not printed or that they were destroyed. This could only be disproved if copies with corner lettering the same as copies from the Imprimatur Sheet are found.

THE STOCK EXCHANGE FORGERY

Early in 1898 forgeries of this stamp were discovered. They emanated from telegraph forms, issued at the London Stock Exchange Post Office, which should have been destroyed. An extensive forgery appears to have successfully defeated the Revenue, because copies dated in June and July 1872 are not uncommon. Probably what happened was that a telegraph clerk substituted forged stamps which he stuck on telegraph forms and pocketed the money he received for genuine ones. The paper of these stamps has no watermark, and the impressions are more blurred than the genuine stamps. Some of the forgeries have impossible corner lettering i.e. subsequent to ' L ', in the N.W. and S.E. corner squares. Similar, but much better, forgeries of Plate 6 are known dated in June 1873. These are much rarer than the forged copies of Plate 5.

Plate 6

Registered February 20, 1869, with Current No. 330, on Spray paper. Put to press March 20, 1872. Otherwise as before.

Plate 7

Registered September 30, 1872, with Current No. · 383, in bright green on Spray paper. Put to press November 11, 1872. Otherwise as before. Copies from this plate exist which are imperforate vertically. They are very rare.

Fifth Issue : September, 1873

Plate 8

This plate, with large coloured letters in corners, was registered September 30, 1872, with Current No. 405, in pale green on Spray paper. Put to press June 10, 1873. The marginal positions of the Plate Number and Current Number were the same as before.

Plate 9

Registered July 10, 1873, with Current No. 425, in bright green on Spray paper. Put to press November 21, 1873. Otherwise as before.

Plate 10

Registered November 25, 1873, with Current No. 436, in deep green on Spray paper. Put to press July 14, 1874. The marginal Plate Number now and hereafter appeared at the N.E. and S.W. corners of the sheet margin, and the Current Number at the N.W. and S.E. corners, instead of as formerly.

Plate 11

Registered April 23, 1874, with Current No. 441, in green on Spray paper. Put to press December 14, 1874. Otherwise as before.

Plate 12

Registered September 30, 1874, with Current No. 456, in bluish green on Spray paper. Put to press June 24, 1875. Otherwise as before. Unused perforated copies in bright blue overprinted SPECIMEN are known. These were probably experimental colour trials.

Plate 13

Registered (in bluish green) April 22, 1875, with Current No. 467, on Spray paper. Put to press January 17, 1876, and 25,000 sheets printed in green.

Sixth Issue : October 14, 1880

Further printings were made from this plate in *orange-brown* on Spray paper. Probably only 5,000 sheets were so printed.

Seventh Issue : June 15, 1881

This plate was re-registered October 21, 1881, with Current No. 467, in pale red-brown on paper with Large Crown watermark, the Imprimatur Sheet being marked ' Proof after alteration of Plate ' [*sic*], although the alteration was in the paper, not the plate. The Large Crown Watermark paper had no marginal

6

PLATE V

1   Die proof of the Ten Pence of July 1867, marked ' Dec. 18 1866 '.

2   Die proof in blue on glazed card of the Two Shillings of July 1867, marked ' Old '.

3   Die proof in blue on glazed card of the Two Shillings with large coloured letters in corners. This proof is marked ' New ' and is inscribed ' Approved 11 March 1872—2280/72 ' in the handwriting of Ormond Hill. This design was not adopted.

4   1866-70. Die proof of the 5 Shillings Die 1 used for Plates 1 and 2. This proof is dated December 21, 1866.

5   Proof of the altered die for the 5 Shillings stamp used for Plate 4. It is inscribed on the front by Ormond Hill, and on the back there is a pencilled note ' I think the alteration satisfactory. J.P.' (Peacock).

1

2

3

4

Aug. 12 1871

approved after alteration 13/8/74

5

PLATE V

Plate Numbers or Current Numbers. The corner lettering of the stamps was the same as before. Copies from this Imprimatur Sheet, as well as from the Imprimatur Sheet in green on Spray paper, were cut, as usual.

The Plate was re-registered again in purple on Large Crown paper on November 3, 1882. In this case it was printed, together with Plate 14, on a double sheet of large Crown paper endorsed ' For change of colour and doubly fugitive ink '.

This printing in purple was made in connection with a series of essays intended for use, but never issued. This series consisted of the Halfpenny (of 1880), One Penny (of 1881), Three Half Pence (of 1880), Two Pence (of 1880), Twopence Halfpenny (Plate 23 of 1881), Three Pence (Plate 21 of 1883), Four Pence (Plate 17 of 1880), Five Pence (of 1881), Six Pence (Plate 18 of 1883) and One Shilling (Plate 14 of 1881). All these were printed in pale lilac on large Crown paper and overprinted with their values in large figures in black, similar to the overprints (in red) of the Three Pence and Six Pence of January 1883. This series of Essays, which is illustrated in the Supplement to *British Isles* under Nos 97 to 106, is very rare. Apparently this ugly method was proposed so as to make use of the lilac ink which was doubly fugitive, as a safeguard against the removal of cancellations ; but the issue of 1883-84 was adopted instead. Copies of Plates 13 and 14 in lilac or purple without the numeral overprint exist, but are usually overprinted SPECIMEN. Without the SPECIMEN overprint they are rare. The watermark, perforation and gum are normal.

Plate 14

Registered (*in green*) December 20, 1875, with Current No. 493, on Spray paper. It was not put to press in green or on Spray paper, but was re-registered in pale red-brown for the Seventh Issue on large Crown paper on October 21, 1881.

It was re-registered again, together with Plate 13 (as mentioned above), in purple on large Crown paper, on November 3, 1882. The marginal positions of the Plate Number and Current Number in green on Spray paper were the same as for Plates 10 to 13.

The Crown paper had no Plate Number or Current Number in the margin. At least one of 'the usual five extra sheets' of Plate 14 in green on Spray paper must have been perforated and issued, because four used copies are known, although no such copy was known to the editors of the *British Philatelist* at the end of 1915, and this was the last of the 'Abnormals' to be discovered. Two (and probably three) of the four recorded copies were used at Greenock. No unused copy is known. It seems probable that all the surviving imperforate copies were cut from the Imprimatur Sheet, since imperforate copies having the same corner letters as specimens from the Imprimatur Sheet have not been recorded. Also, as only four perforated specimens are known, and all these would seem to be from the same sheet, it seems probable that, of the sheets printed for registration purposes in green on Spray paper, only one sheet, apart from the Imprimatur, survived, and that this supplied the only four known perforated specimens. These were perforated by the official comb machine, leaving gutter margins.

Chapter Fourteen

Surface-Printed Stamps: 1855 to 1883

TWO SHILLINGS

First Issue : July 1, 1867

Plate 1

Registered April 5, 1867, with Current No. 285, in light blue on Spray paper. Put to press April 10, 1867. The issued stamps range in shade from pale milky-blue to very dark blue, and there is a scarce cobalt shade. As originally registered the plate was out of square. This was corrected and it was re-registered on July 5, 1867. There were large white corner letters and the Plate Number was on both sides of the stamps. The plate consisted of 240 stamps, in twelve panes disposed in four horizontal rows of three, each pane containing 20 stamps in five horizontal rows of four. The corner lettering ran across the plate, in the usual manner from A A-A A to L T-T L. The marginal Plate Number is above the penultimate stamp in the top row and below the second stamp in the bottom row. The Current Number is above the second stamp in the top row and below the penulti-mate stamp in the bottom row. Through carelessness, some of the stamps were issued at Hull on June 17, 1867, if not earlier. Probably 2,005 sheets were printed from the plate as originally registered out of square. Imperforate used specimens are recorded by Wright and Creeke, which indicates that at least one sheet was issued accidentally imperforate. There exist also the usual imperforate copies cut from the Imprimatur Sheet.

Second Issue : February, 1880

In February 1880 the colour was changed to light brown. Only 1,000 sheets were printed in this colour. Of these $657\frac{7}{12}$ sheets were destroyed, and in July 1880 only $4\frac{1}{4}$ sheets were left in stock. There was no Imprimatur Sheet in brown, and im-perforate copies are not recorded ; but some exist in unused condition, including at least one block. One of the Editors has a mint block of sixteen perforated very badly. This may have been employed for the trial of a perforating machine or it may be a portion of a discarded sheet not intended for issue. Perforated copies with SPECIMEN overprint also exist. The Authorities at Somerset House evidently retained some sheets, and must have left at least one imperforate from which copies were cut. There is a fairly good forgery of this stamp lettered HB-BH, but the colour is too yellow. Sperati made facsimiles of these stamps, usually with forged cancellations.

Plate 2

Was never registered or put to press.

Plate 3

Registered January 23, 1867, with Current No. 298, in light blue on Spray paper. This plate was never put to press. Wright and Creeke assumed that ' the usual five extra sheets ' were printed, put into stock and issued, from the fact that used perforated copies are well known ; and one such unused copy has been recorded. As copies are very rare, it is possible that not all the spare sheets were perforated. If they were, all the imperforate copies would be those cut from the Imprimatur Sheet. In this case again the vertical perforation was alongside the stamps in all cases, leaving no imperforate ' gutter ' margin, as was normal for the sheets from Plate 1. The make-up of the sheet, and marginal positions of the Plate Number and Current Number, were the same as for Plate 1.

In December 1872 a new die was made for this value, proofs from which exist ; but no plate was made from this. It provided for coloured letters in the corner squares.

FIVE SHILLINGS

First Issue : July 1, 1867

Plate 1

Registered and put to press April 18, 1867, with Current No. 284, in pink on paper watermarked Maltese Cross. The plate consisted of 80 stamps in four panes of 20 stamps in four horizontal rows of five each. The white corner lettering runs from A A-AA to JH-HJ. The Plate Number appeared once in white on each stamp. The marginal Plate Number appeared in the N.E. and S.W. corners of the sheet, and the Current Number in the N.W. and S.E. corners. The perforation was $15\frac{1}{2} \times 15$. No question of ' the usual five extra sheets ' arises because printing began at the date of registration. Imperforate copies are recorded as having been issued thus, and, as usual, imperforate specimens cut from the Imprimatur Sheet exist.

Plate 2

Registered July 5, 1867, with Current No. 294, in pale rose on Maltese Cross paper. Put to press March 25, 1874—nearly seven years after registration. If ' the usual five extra sheets ' were printed for registration purposes, and these were perforated and issued (evidence concerning which is lacking) any copy from this plate dated prior to March 1874 would be from these. But none such has been recorded ; nor any imperforate specimen, other than the copies cut from the Imprimatur Sheet. The marginal positions of the Plate Number and Current Number were the same as for Plate 1.

Plate 3

This plate was not registered or put to press.

Second Issue : November, 1882

Plate 4

Registered November 28, 1874, with Current No. 454, in carmine-pink, *on Maltese Cross paper*. This plate was not put to press on Maltese Cross paper. A new die was made for this plate which differed slightly from Die 1, and the plate was cut down in size to consist of 56 stamps in one pane of seven horizontal rows of eight, lettered from AA-AA to HG-GH. It was re-registered thus on slightly blued Large Anchor paper on October 24, 1862, nearly eight years after original registration. The second Imprimatur Sheet was endorsed ' Alteration in size of plate ' and ' Ordered - that the plate, as altered, be brought into use '. The Plate Number and Current Number did not appear in the margin. The perforation was 14. Issued copies on the large Anchor fiscal paper are sometimes blued to a greater or lesser degree. Wright and Creeke assumed that ' the usual five extra sheets ' on Maltese Cross paper were printed for registration purposes, but no perforated or used copies have been recorded, and it seems probable that the only specimens on this paper which exist are the imperforate copies cut from the Imprimatur Sheet.

TEN SHILLINGS

First Issue : September 26, 1878

Plate 1

Registered and put to press August 6, 1878, with Current No. 559, in green-grey on Maltese Cross paper. The plate consisted of 80 stamps of four panes of 20 stamps in four horizontal rows of five each. The white corner lettering runs from A A-A A to J H-H J. The Plate Number appeared once on each stamp. The Marginal Plate Number appeared in the N.E. and S.W. corners of the sheet and the Current Number in the N.W. and S.E. corners. The perforation was $15\frac{1}{2} \times 15$. There appears to have been only one printing (3,025 sheets) of this stamp on Maltese Cross paper. The only imperforate copies which exist would seem to be those cut from the Imprimatur Sheet. There was a series of imperforate colour trials on normal paper overprinted SPECIMEN.

Second Issue : February 1883

The plate was altered to consist of only 56 stamps in one pane of seven horizontal rows of eight, lettered from A A-A A to H G-G H. It was re-registered thus on January 27, 1883, on blued paper with Large Anchor watermark, and the Imprimatur Sheet was endorsed ' Proof after alteration in size of plate '. The Plate Number and Current Number did not appear in the margin. The perforation was 14. Issued copies are usually on more or less blued paper. Unused copies on really white paper

are very rare.   There is a good forgery lettered **EB-BE**, which
appears to be on genuine Anchor paper with genuine perforation,
but the colour is more grey than greyish-green.   Imperforate
copies cut from the (re-registered) Imprimatur Sheet exist.

ONE POUND

First Issue: September 1878

Plate 1

Registered and put to press August 6, 1878, with Current No.
558, in brown-violet on Maltese Cross paper.   The plate consisted of 80 stamps in four panes of 20 stamps in four horizontal
rows of five each.   The white corner lettering runs from A A-A A
to J H-H J.   The Plate Number appeared once on each stamp.
The Marginal Plate Number appeared in the N.E. and S.W.
corners of the sheet, and the Current Number in the N.W. and
S.E. corners.   The perforation was $15\frac{1}{2} \times 15$.   There appears to
have been only one printing (3,025 sheets) of this stamp on Maltese
Cross paper.   The only imperforate copies which exist would
seem to be those cut from the Imprimatur Sheet.   There was
a series of imperforate colour trials on normal paper overprinted
SPECIMEN.

Second Issue : December, 1882

The plate was altered to consist of 56 stamps in one pane of
seven horizontal rows of eight, lettered from A A-A A to H G-G H.
It was re-registered thus on November 20, 1882, on blued paper
with Large Anchor watermark and the Imprimatur Sheet was
endorsed ' Alteration in size of plate ' and ' Ordered - That the
plate, as altered, be brought into use '.   The Plate Number
and Current Number did not appear in the margin.   The perforation was 14.   Issued copies are on more or less blued paper.
The Editors have no record of an unused copy on really white
paper.   Apparently 2,000 sheets only were printed.   Imperforate copies cut from the (re-registered) Imprimatur Sheet exist.

PLATE VI

1 1878. Ten Shillings die proof of the first state. The web outside the lower ornaments connecting the lower letter squares is not cleared. This proof is dated April 26, 1878.

2 Second state with web cleared. Dated May 1, 1878.

3 Third state. Ornaments above T and G of ' Postage ' and below S and I of ' Shillings ' have been amended. Dated May 2, 1878.

4 Fourth and final state. The top and bottom lines of background have been altered to run parallel with the others. Dated May 4, 1878, and marked ' Before hardening '.

5 Die proof of the One Pound stamp before the surround was cut away. Dated April 18, 1878.

6 Die proof of the One Pound stamp issued September 1878.

1

2

3

4

5

6

PLATE VI

FIVE POUNDS

Only Issue : March 21, 1882

Plate 1

Registered March 9, 1882, with Current No. 526, in orange-vermilion, on blued paper, with watermark two Large Anchors. Although not registered until March, it appears to have been put to press at the end of January or early in February 1882. The Imprimatur Sheet was endorsed ' This Plate has already been registered by the Secretary's Department as a Telegraph Plate. The word " Telegraph " [*sic*] has since been cut out, and the word " Postage " is now printed in the space, to render the stamps available for either telegraph or postal purposes ' ; and ' Ordered - That the plate, as altered, be brought into use '. The plate comprised 56 stamps in two vertically disposed panes, each of seven horizontal rows of four in a row. Neither the Plate Number nor the Current Number appeared in the margin. Two large Anchor watermarks appeared on each stamp. The Plate Number was in both the top corner squares. The white corner letters in the lower corners run from AA to DN. The first letter denotes the position of the stamp in the horizontal row ; and the second the number of the row. The first printing was in dull brownish orange-vermilion, and the paper was markedly blued. Subsequent printings showed less and less orange and less blued paper, until the colour was bright vermilion and the paper quite white. The perforation was 14. Imperforate copies which exist were presumably cut from the Imprimatur Sheet. Wright and Creeke include this stamp under the Issues of 1881-84 (S.G. Nos. 170 to 196) ; but it is included here under the Issues of 1867-83 because it forms part of the series with white corner letters, and appears as S.G. No. 137.

Chapter Fifteen

The 1880 to 1881 Issue

Halfpenny :	Pale to Deep Green
One Penny :	Venetian Red
Three Half Pence :	Venetian Red
Two Pence :	Pale to Deep Rose
Five Pence :	Indigo

Printed by De La Rue on paper watermarked Imperial Crown perforated 14 by comb machine in two vertical panes, each of 120 impressions.

Halfpenny

This, the first surface printed stamp of this value, was taken from one of the essays submitted by the printers when they tendered for the One Penny issued some months earlier, and was, with the Three Half Pence value, one of the two first stamps issued without any corner lettering.

Four plates, numbered 1, 2, 3 and 6 were certainly used for this issue, and possibly Nos 7 and 8 were also employed, but Nos 5 and 6 were spoiled in the making and discarded. No plate number appeared on this or any subsequent issues, but a record was kept by marking the number on the side margins of the Imprimatur Sheets.

The stamp was issued on October 17, 1880, in a deep green colour which in course of time varied to a dull pale green.

One Penny

The contract for both the Halfpenny and One Penny stamps, which Perkins Bacon & Co had held for so many years, was to end at the close of 1879, and in anticipation of this some six firms were approached to tender for a new contract. Perkins Bacon submitted many designs, De La Rue several, whilst those from other printers were apparently examples of their work rather than actual designs for stamps.

De La Rue obtained the contract, and die proofs are known of over twenty designs submitted by them, with various types of the Queen's head, before one with the usual Wyon style of head was approved. (*See* Plate VII.)

As many as thirty-three plates were made for the stamp, but only eighteen were put to press. Plate 3 was damaged, Plate 11 never registered and Plates 6, 16, 21, 22 and 25 to 30 never used.

The lettering followed the old procedure A A to T L, but without any plate number on the stamp. The margins also were blank, so did not show either a plate or a control number.

Essays exist showing small black circles between the two panes of a sheet of this value, but this idea was never utilised, and was considered to be an experiment for Indian issues.

The stamp was first put on sale on January 1, 1880, and had a life of only a little over eighteen months. The shades of Venetian red vary very little, although two sheets have been found in decidedly deeper colourings. Imperforate copies are known, but no colour trials have so far been recorded. This and all the other values of this series were printed in a fugitive ink.

Three Halfpence

This stamp, like the line-engraved one it superseded, was issued in the same colour as the One Penny in use at the time, namely in venetian-red, but owing to the design the colour does not appear so dense. It came into use on October 14, 1880, and only two plates were made and put to press.

Two Pence

This value was issued on December 8, 1880, in pale rose. Later the colour was deeper and, in fact, became quite deep before the stamp went out of issue. Only two plates were prepared and used.

Five Pence

Issued March 15, 1881, to defray the new postage rate to India and China. The shades of this value in indigo vary very slightly.

Colour trials, printed in twenty-four different colours on white paper, and a few on coloured paper, were taken of the Three Halfpence, Two Pence and Five Pence, and, at the same time, of all other values then in use, other than the Halfpenny and One Penny.

1881 : ONE PENNY LILAC

(i) Fourteen dots in each corner

On Crown Watermarked paper, perforated 14 (comb), printed in two vertical panes each of 120 impressions.

The Customs and Inland Revenue Act of 1881 having abolished the distinction between one penny stamps employed separately for postage and revenue, a stamp was required to meet all purposes. The design had to bear the new inscription ' Postage and Revenue ' and it was decided to print this value in a doubly fugitive ink, hence the change of colour to lilac.

Eight plates in all were constructed and the stamp came into use on July 12. The colour both of this and its successor was officially called purple, but is what is generally known as lilac, varying only slightly in shade. No colour trials are recorded.

(ii) Sixteen dots in each corner

For some reason Die 1 of the above was soon discarded and a second one was brought into use during the same year. It was somewhat different from the earlier die, as not only were sixteen dots placed in each of the four corners, but the lettering also was slightly larger. A considerable number of plates were made from this die and probably from successors which are indistinguishable from it. The first of these plates was put to press on October 14, 1881. The earliest date known for the actual issue was December 12 in the same year.

The shades of the so-called ' purple ' colour are numerous, namely, light to dark lilac, reddish lilac, and a deepish purple. The margins of the sheets were quite plain until 1884, when a sans-serif control letter was placed under the last stamp but

one on the sheet, and this was changed in alphabetical sequence
about twice every year.   It was done to facilitate booking methods
at headquarters.

A so-called error, which however proved to be intentional,
occurred some years later when a few sheets were issued with the
N control cancelled by two coloured bars and the letter O printed
by its side.

According to Wright and Creeke, the second letter and the
cancelling bars were printed at the same time, but the variation
in the position of the O and bars in relation to the N does not
bear this out.

From May 1887 a line of printer's rule was placed round each
of the two panes on the sheet to relieve the edges of the plates
from the pressure which, in printing, always falls more heavily
on those parts.   A further addition was made later, namely,
a row of forty-eight short vertical line-blocks or pillars, between
the panes, the sudden break between which sometimes caused
the adjoining horizontal rows to become defective.

The ' Jubilee ' line and control varieties are :

A to J without line.

G to W, including the cancelled N with O, with line.

W and X with line and central line-blocks.

The above varieties can be further sub-divided according to
the way in which the sheets were perforated, i.e. whether they
were inserted in the perforation machine top or bottom first,
and in consequence vertically perforated or imperforate where the
control is found.

In addition to the foregoing the following varieties must
also be recorded :

(a) Printed on both sides of the paper.

(b) Printed on back of the paper over the gum.

(c) Imperforate or partly so.

(d) Bottom frame line thicker than one above and broken
under E and PE of *One Penny*.

(e) On blue ' safety ' paper.

(*f*) On laid or repp, instead of wove, paper (found only in latest printings).

(*g*) Bottom frame line damaged and repaired on second stamp in top row of upper pane on sheet with Control S.

(*h*) Double marginal line above top row in upper pane.

(*i*) Right hand vertical frame line broken on last stamp in penultimate row of Sheet with Control X.

This stamp is also known bisected and used with two whole stamps of the same value to pay the $2\frac{1}{2}$d rate to America. This procedure, although passed by the postal authorities, was never sanctioned.

Colour trials both on white and coloured paper are numerous, and exist both imperforate and perforated.

Chapter Sixteen

The 1883 to 1884 Issue

THE HIGH VALUES

2 Shillings & 6 Pence :	lilac on blue paper
2 Shillings & 6 Pence :	lilac on white paper
2 Shillings & 6 Pence :	deep lilac on white paper
Five Shillings :	rose on blue paper
Five Shillings :	rose on white paper
Five Shillings :	carmine on white paper
Ten Shillings :	ultramarine on blue paper
Ten Shillings :	cobalt on blue paper
Ten Shillings :	cobalt on white paper
Ten Shillings :	ultramarine on white paper
Ten Shillings :	pale ultramarine on white paper

Letters in all four corners. Printed by De La Rue on wove paper watermarked Large Anchor, perforated 14, in sheets of 112 impressions arranged in two vertical panes of 56 in 8 rows of 7 each.

The blue paper referred to above is that previously employed for the fiscal stamps which had now been discontinued.

Two Shillings and Sixpence

Issued July 2, 1883, as it was then found necessary to provide stamps of this and higher values for postal, telegraph, and the usual revenue services, more particularly for the last two; hence the printing at first on the usual blue fiscal paper.

Two plates, both unnumbered, were prepared and registered on June 19, 1883. The lilac colour varies very little, but the blueing ranges from a deep to a light shade.

Early in 1884 the paper used was changed to white, and remained so during the life of this series, but the stamp itself varied from a palish to a quite deep lilac.

Five Shillings

This value was introduced on April 1, 1884. Two plates were employed, having been registered on September 6, 1883. It was first printed on blue paper, but before long appeared on the usual white paper. During the use of the latter the colour of the printing was changed from rose to crimson.

Ten Shillings

This altered design for this value was placed on issue on April 1, 1884, the two plates made and used having been registered on July 17 and August 1 of the previous year. It was printed in the first instance on blue paper, and is found in both ultramarine and cobalt colourings, but the number issued in the latter must have been small judging by its scarcity.

When the paper was changed to white the cobalt colour was the first used, and this indicates that ultramarine was chosen in the first case for the printings on the blue paper. The authorities however soon reverted to ultramarine and the stamp can be found in many shades of this.

1884 to 1888: ONE POUND

One Pound : brown-lilac on white paper watermarked three Imperial Crowns.

One Pound : brown-lilac on white paper watermarked three Orbs.

The design and oblong shape of this stamp was taken from the One Pound Telegraph stamp of 1877 which had become obsolete at the close of the year 1881.

Two plates were prepared, each consisting of two vertical panes of 40 impressions in horizontal rows of four, without any marginal inscriptions and the lettering running from A A A A to D T T D. The first plate was approved on January 31, 1884, and put to press two days later, whilst the second plate registered on February 25, 1884, was brought into use on that day.

The stamps were issued on April 1 on Crown Watermarked paper, three Crowns to each impression, but in February 1888 it appeared on paper showing three Orb watermarks instead of the Crowns. This was due to a mistake when ordering a fresh supply of paper. Being in use for a considerably less time than that watermarked with the Crowns, it is an appreciably rarer stamp.

The second plate for this value being broken showed a flaw on the stamp lettered CJ/JC, two breaks being found repaired in the outer frame line of the oval below the words of value.

A further flaw is found on the stamp AT/TA, the right-lower corner of the bottom T-square joining the ornamentation below the left figure of value ; it was repaired later.

The colour was changed to green and so issued on January 27, 1891. As the same varieties exist as are found in the brown stamp, it is evident that the same plate was used to start with, and before any correction had been undertaken. A new plate, the third, was registered in this green colour on November 26, 1890, and very shortly afterwards put into use.

A lithographed forgery of this stamp is well known.

1883 to 1884 : THE LOW VALUES

Halfpenny :	slate blue
Three Halfpence :	lilac
Two Pence :	lilac
Two Pence Halfpenny :	lilac
Three Pence :	lilac
Four Pence :	dull green
Five Pence :	dull green
Six Pence :	dull green
Nine Pence :	dull green
One Shilling :	dull green

On Imperial Crown Watermarked paper, perforated 14

Except for the Halfpenny stamp only two colours were used for this issue, the authorities having decided, in order to avoid the danger of cleaning, to print all the values in doubly fugitive inks, and only lilac and dull green colours would meet this requirement.

PLATE VII

1   Alternative design with ' Postage One Penny ' blacked out. This design was submitted in May 1879.

2   Die proof of the approved head.

3   Die proof of a further alternative design for the One Penny of 1880.

4   Die proof of a further design with head Type 3 and Imperial crown.

5   Die proof of head Type 3.

6   Die proofs of further designs for the One Penny of 1880 with
7   head Type 2.

8 to 11

Die proofs of further essays for the One Penny of 1880 with head Type 4. These were submitted by De La Rue in this form. Figure 9, but without corner letters and simplified, was used for the frame for the Halfpenny value.

1

2

3

4

5

6

7

8

9

10

11

PLATE VII

The Halfpenny issued in slate-blue was exactly the same as that of October 1880, except for the change in colour which was presumably made so that it was distinct from the higher values of the same series.   In any case, as it was not required for revenue purposes, there was no need for it to be printed in fugitive ink to avoid the danger of the stamps being cleaned.   Colour trials were taken before the colour was settled and these can be found both imperforate and perforated.

The Ninepence being required urgently to defray new postal rates was issued on August 1, 1883, and all the other values appeared on April 1, 1884.

Only two plates were constructed for the four lower values from Three Halfpence to Three Pence, and for the Six Pence and One Shilling.   For the Four Pence three were made, but only two used ;   and for the Nine Pence four were provided, although the first two were never used as the lettering was faulty.   The original die for the Five Pence, from which two plates had been made, cracked early in use and was discarded.   All the stamps already printed from these plates were supposed to have been destroyed, but a few copies, all unused, are known to have survived and are consequently rare.   A new die was called for and, as it was realised in time that the original value tablet did not conform to those of the other values, it was noticeably modified.   In the original die the five was an ordinary Arabic numeral and the ' d ' was lower case roman with a line below it, whilst in the replaced die the figure five was the same thickness throughout and the ' d ' was lower case sans-serif with a dot below it. (*See* Plate IX.)

The usual two plates were made from this second die and constructed in the same way as for the Half Penny, Three Half-pence, Two Pence, Four Pence, and One Shilling values, namely in two panes of 120 impressions one above the other on the sheet.

In the case of the Two Pence, Twopence Halfpenny, Six Pence and Nine Pence stamps the two panes were placed side by side on account of their different shape.   The sheets of both types of setting had plain margins.

Stamps perforated 12 instead of 14 are known in all values, both with and without SPECIMEN overprint ; in the latter state they are extremely rare. They were never issued and were so perforated only for trial purposes at Somerset House.

This 1883-84 issue had been in use only for a very short time before serious complaints were made by post office employees, who pointed out that once a stamp had been cancelled it was frequently impossible to tell whether the right rate had been paid or not.

The general public also voiced their objections and in consequence of this outcry a Committee was appointed to study the whole question. The Government printers, De La Rue, were called in to make suggestions, and as a result they, with the assistance of outsiders, prepared a hundred or more essays for consideration. Some were bi-coloured and others were prepared on various coloured papers in order to make each value as distinctive as possible. The Committee decided to use both of these ideas, and to keep to the usual shape for all values up to One Shilling. The eventual outcome of all this was the ' Jubilee ' issue of 1887. The colour trials of the 1883-84 issue, made for the above Committee, must have been numerous and well distributed considering the number in circulation, but very few copies of any of the actual designs submitted passed out of the printers' hands.

Chapter Seventeen

The 1887 to 1900 Issues

Jubilee Issue on paper watermarked Imperial Crown, Perforated 14

One Halfpenny :	vermilion on white
One Halfpenny :	blue green (April 17, 1900)
1½d :	dull purple and green on white
2d :	green and vermilion on white
2d :	green and carmine on white
2½d :	purple on blue paper
3d :	purple on yellow paper
3d :	purple on orange
4d :	green and purple brown
4½d :	green and carmine
5d :	dull purple and blue
6d :	purple on rose-red paper
9d :	dull purple and blue
10d :	dull purple and carmine (February 24, 1890)
One Shilling :	green
One Shilling :	green and carmine (July 11, 1900)

For this issue the head of Queen Victoria was reduced in size, and although several head dies were used for the different values, it is difficult, if not impossible, to detect any variation between them.

The stamps, except where mentioned later, were as usual printed in two vertical panes of 120, and the margins, except for division ornaments, were quite plain for the first printings of every value, except the 4½d and 10d issued later.

ONE HALFPENNY VERMILION

After the initial printing a control letter, as had been introduced for use on the sheets of the current One Penny lilac, was placed in the bottom margin under the last stamp but one in the lower pane, and some little while after this the Jubilee line,

PLATE VIII

Essays prepared by De La Rue for an issue proposed for 1883.
This set is the one illustrated in the Appendix to *History of the
Adhesive Stamps of the British Isles*, by H. B. Wright and A. B.
Creeke.

The stamps are in lilac with black surcharges.

PLATE VIII

previously described, was added to all further plates that were brought into use.

The printings with no control and with control letter ' A ' have no Jubilee line round the panes, whilst printings with control letters ' B ' to ' E ' appeared both with and without Jubilee line. Normally the Jubilee line is rounded at the corners of each pane, but certain of the printings with control letters ' D ' to ' F ' have the line square at the corners and there is a sub-variety of the square corner having the vertical line bevelled off.

In the square corner variety, whether bevelled or not, there is a small gap between the vertical and horizontal lines of rule. Printings with control letters ' G ' to ' Q ' have the Jubilee line extending all round the panes and rounded at each corner. There are no line blocks between the panes.

(a) No Jubilee line,   no control.
(b) No Jubilee line,   controls ' A ' to ' E '.
(c) With Jubilee line, rounded at corners, controls ' B ' to ' Q '.
(d) With Jubilee line, square at corners, controls ' D ' to ' F '.
(e) With Jubilee line, square, but vertical line bevelled at corners, controls ' D ' to ' F '.

Bottom right hand corner blocks or pairs with no control are scarce, as also are controls ' A ' to ' D ' with no Jubilee line.

Control ' B ' with the line and control ' E ' without it are very rare, and controls ' D ' to ' F ' with line square at corners, bevelled or not, are very scarce. Sheets without control and with controls ' A ' to ' E ' with no Jubilee line, and control ' B ' with line, only exist with bottom margin perforated, but the others exist both with margins perforated and imperforate. Some of these with imperforate margins are scarce.

This value printed in vermilion is known with ' Pears Soap ' advertisement printed on the back. It is also known printed on the back over the gum.

ONE HALFPENNY BLUISH-GREEN

The colour of the halfpenny value was changed to a bluish-green in 1900 and appears only with ' R ' control, rounded at the corners. Some printings have no pillars between the two vertical panes and others have them. The bottom margin is found both perforated and imperforate. Copies with inverted watermark exist.

Colour trials in varying shades of green, closely resembling the selected one, were perforated 14.

A rare variety of this value is that printed on the gummed side of the paper.

THREE HALFPENCE

When this was first issued, both colours were pale shades of dull purple and green, but some later printings were much deeper, this being particularly noticeable in the second state of the plates.

There are three marginal settings, namely :

(*a*) With no Jubilee line.

(*b*) With purple and green lines continuous all round each pane.

(*c*) With continuous purple lines as before, but green lines at the sides only.

Corner and middle blocks with no Jubilee line or with both coloured lines all round the panes are not common.

On this and all higher values there is no control letter on the sheets.

Copies are known with the watermark inverted.

TWOPENCE

The green colour used for all but the value tablet, which was in carmine or the scarcer vermilion, varies very little in shade.

An essay exists in which the value tablet has a solid background, and some thirty to forty different colour trials of the approved designs are known.

The three marginal settings are :

(*a*) With no Jubilee line.

(*b*) With green and carmine (or vermilion) lines continuous all round each pane.

(*c*) With continuous green lines all round, and short carmine (or vermilion) lines opposite the value tablets at the top and bottom and at the sides of each pane. The short lines are sometimes very faint and occasionally non-existent.

Marginal variety (*b*) is very rare. Only a few sheets of this variety were issued in December 1889 and January 1890.

TWOPENCE HALFPENNY

This appears to have been the only stamp of the series the design of which troubled the authorities, as some nine essays were submitted to Her Majesty before one met with her approval. They were all in purple on blue paper and the only set known is still in the printers' hands.

Very few colour trials in the approved design were taken. There are three marginal settings :

(*a*) With no Jubilee lines.
(*b*) With continuous purple lines round each pane.
(*c*) As last, but pillars added between the upper and lower panes of each Post Office sheet.

Blocks showing portions of two panes without pillars between them are elusive.

THREEPENCE

Because of the decidedly yellow paper the purple printing of this value has a lightish brown appearance.

A printing was issued in 1891 on a deepish orange-yellow paper, but as such stamps are scarce the supply must have been a very small one.

The marginal settings are exactly the same as those used for the 2½d stamps, and so do not need a detailed description.

Only a few different colour trials were taken.

This stamp can be found with the overprint ' Railway Letter Stamp ' in three different types, but they are only essays, as they were never employed for that purpose.

PLATE IX

1   1883-84. Proof from the rejected die marked ' 26 Feb. 83. Before hardening.' Two plates were prepared from this die and six reams of stamps printed from them, but they were never issued and all the sheets, except presumably one, were destroyed.

2   First ' Duty ' die for the Five Pence value of 1887. This was used for the first two printings, both of which had plain margins round the panes. This proof is marked ' 13 Aug. 86. Before hardening.'

3   Proof of the second ' Duty ' die which was used for the third printing on August 10, 1888, and subsequent printings. These had jubilee lines round the panes. Proof marked ' 9 Nov. 86. Before hardening.'

4   First state of the Tenpence of February 24, 1890. Short lined vertical blocks at base and long blocks at side. This piece is from the N.E. pane of thé Post Office sheet—the right side of the Mill sheet.

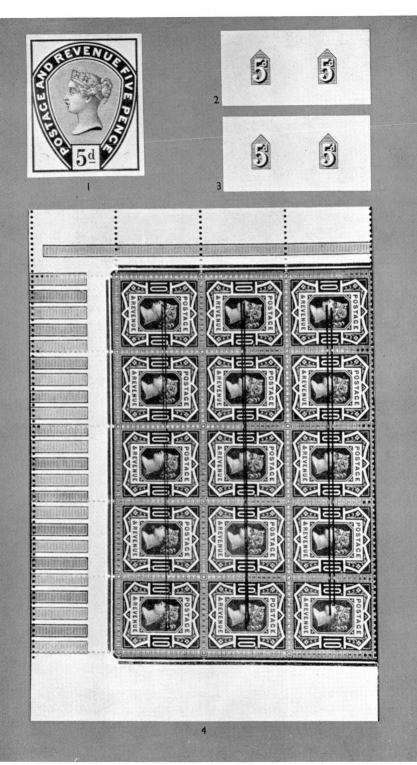

PLATE IX

FOURPENCE

Of the two colours used for this stamp only the purple varies to any extent; in some printings it is almost a purple-brown.

In order to understand properly the marginal settings of this value it is necessary to remember that it did not conform to the usual make-up, but was printed in mill sheets of 320 impressions, divided into 16 panes of 20 stamps. Each mill sheet was divided horizontally and vertically into four Post Office sheets before issue, making four sheets of four panes each.

The settings are :

(a) No Jubilee lines and all margins plain, but a large watermark ' Postage ' can be clearly seen across the vertical panes of the four-pane sheets.

(b) No Jubilee lines, but below each upper pane and above each lower pane on each Post Office sheet there are two long horizontal line-blocks, one brown and one green, the brown one in each case being nearer to the stamps. In addition, there are, between each horizontal pane, twenty-one short horizontal blocks, alternately green and brown (the top and bottom blocks are always green) making eleven green and ten brown blocks.

(c) Similar to setting (b) except that there are continuous green and brown Jubilee lines all round each pane, and the number of short blocks between each horizontal pane is increased to twenty-three.

(d) Similar to setting (c) except that the green Jubillee line round each pane is cut away at each corner and thirty-seven thin horizontal alternate green and brown lines are added in the left and right hand margins of each Post Office sheet.

(e) Similar to setting (d) except that the thin horizontal green and brown lines to left and right of the sheet are omitted. There is a very rare variety of this setting, showing portions of two unsevered Post Office sheets, which proves that abnormally the mill sheet as printed was not always divided into four Post Office sheets before use. Only two specimens of this variety are known.

Complete panes or even large blocks, showing marginal settings (*a*), (*b*), and (*c*) are rare, and setting (*d*) in similar condition is scarce.

Due probably to faulty inking or worn plates this fourpenny stamp can be found with no colouring matter at all in the centre of the figure 4. Often one of two of the fours on a stamp show this fault, but copies where all four do so are far from common.

The last setting of this value is known printed on laid or repp paper. No colour trials are recorded. Copies are known with inverted watermark.

FOURPENCE HALFPENNY

This stamp did not appear until September 1892 and was printed like the 4d in sheets of 320 impressions, divided into sixteen panes of 20 stamps, with marginal setting corresponding to setting (*e*) of the 4d.

A large number of colour trials exist, often in vertical pairs imperforate between to show off the coloured surround of the stamps. They are also known with trial cancellations.

FIVEPENCE

The make-up of the sheets corresponds with that of the 2d and the marginal varieties were similar.

For the value tablets two different dies were employed, varying very slightly from one another. Die 1 was used throughout the first setting and Die 2 for the other two. (*See* Plate IX.)

The marginal varieties thus are :

(*a*) No Jubilee line. Die 1 value tablet.

(*b*) With Jubilee lines both blue and purple round the panes, with Die 2 value tablet.

(*c*) With purple lines all round the panes and short broken blue lines arranged as described for the last setting of the 2d. Die 2 value tablet.

Marginal blocks with no Jubilee lines (*a*) and with continuous lines round the panes are scarce.

No colour trials appear to have been taken.

SIXPENCE

The purple colour on the rose-red paper varies in depth, the deeper printings being more noticeable after the Jubilee line was added round the stamps.

The set-up of the sheets is similar to the $2\frac{1}{2}$d value, namely :

(a) No Jubilee line round the two panes of 120 impressions.

(b) With Jubilee lines.

(c) With Jubilee lines and pillars between the two panes.

Blocks showing portions of two panes without pillars between them are far from common.

Colour trials exist, but are not numerous.

An embossed die, and proofs of it, are known for this stamp, but there is no evidence to show why this was prepared.

NINEPENCE

Except in the last printing, where softer and lighter shades of both the purple and green colours are found, there is little variation in the printing.

The make up of the mill sheet is exactly the same as in the case of the 4d value. For this value, however, each mill sheet was broken up into sixteen separate panes before issue to the Post Offices until near the end of the issue, when sheets of four panes each were issued as in the case of the 4d. In consequence anything larger than a pane of the first three settings should not exist.

There are four marginal settings :

(a) No Jubilee lines and all margins plain.

(b) No Jubilee lines, but purple and blue pillars between the panes, similar to those in setting (b) of the 4d.

(c) Purple and blue Jubilee lines round each pane, purple lines cut away at the corners and pillars between the panes, also thin horizontal lines at the outer sides of the panes, all exactly the same as in setting (d) of the 4d.

(d) Similar to setting (c) but without the thin outer horizontal lines.

Large blocks showing settings (*a*) and (*b*) are scarce and setting (*c*) is rare.   The last setting can be found on laid or repp paper. No colour trials appear to exist.

TENPENCE

No very noticeable change of shade is found in this purple and carmine stamp, first issued on February 24, 1890.   The set-up was similar to the 9d, but a plate consisted of only four panes of 20 impressions each.

Originally the stamps were issued only in single panes, but towards the end they came out in complete sheets of four panes.

There are only two marginal settings :

(*a*) Continuous purple and carmine Jubilee lines round each pane, cut away at the corners ; one long purple line-block running vertically along the inner side of each pane, and twenty-three short vertical pillars between each upper and lower pane.   (*See* Plate IX.)

(*b*) Jubilee lines and pillars exactly similar to those of setting (*e*) of the 4d.

Setting (*a*), especially in complete panes, is exceedingly rare. This value exists on laid or repp paper, like the 4d and 9d.

Colour trials of this value are numerous, both on white and coloured papers ; also with dated obliterations.

Copies are known with inverted watermark.

ONE SHILLING

First issued in green, and in the standard setting of two vertical panes of 120 impressions each.

The stamp can be found in both dull green and a brighter grey-green, but the latter is less common.

Copies are known with inverted watermark.

There are only two marginal settings :

(*a*) Without Jubilee line.

(*b*) With green Jubilee line round each pane.

On July 11, 1900, a bi-coloured shilling stamp was substituted. This had a carmine border, and the centre vignette in the original colour. The object of the change was to distinguish the One Shilling from the Halfpenny value, which had been changed to green some three months earlier in order to conform to the Universal Postal Union scheme, which stipulated that the same colours were to be used for certain stamps of equivalent values in the different countries which had joined the Union.

The only setting for this bi-coloured stamp consisted of continuous carmine and green Jubilee lines round the panes, except that the green line is cut away at the corners. Colour trials of both issues, perforated, are numerous. There are fifteen different examples in single colours and eighteen in bi-colours.

8

Chapter Eighteen

Issues of King Edward VII

QUEEN VICTORIA died on January 22, 1901. For more than sixty years her portrait as a young woman had appeared on all the stamps of the United Kingdom and most of those of the British Empire. This portrait is associated with an era of social scientific and mechanical progress greater and more rapid than that of any corresponding period in history, an era during which the Empire reached the apex of its prestige and prosperity.

The Authorities consulted De La Rue about the new issue of stamps, and the first essays consisted of the frames of the then current Halfpenny, One Penny, 1½d, 2d, 2½d, 3d, 4d, 5d, 6d, 9d 10d and One Shilling values, with the head of King Edward VII substituted lithographically for that of the Queen. (*See* Plate XI.)

Four sets of these essays were prepared, each showing the King's head facing differently. For the 1½d, 2d, 3d, 4d, 5d, 9d, 10d and One Shilling, designs and colours similar to those of the Victorian stamps were approved ; but a crown was incorporated above the King's portrait and other alterations were included in most of the designs. For the Half Penny, One Penny, 2½d and Six Pence an entirely new design was prepared, and the colours of the Half Penny, One Penny and 2½d were changed to green, red, and blue respectively to conform with Universal Postal Union requirements. The colour chosen for the Six Pence was purple, the fugitive ink of which was considered most suitable for stamps used largely on contracts with pen cancellations.

The portrait adopted for the stamps was executed by Emil Fuchs, an Austrian, and the selection of a foreign artist for this purpose caused criticism. It was explained, however, that the King himself had chosen the portrait and given the artist a sitting to enable him to adapt this for the special requirements of the stamps, which necessitated a head in two different sizes. Fuchs also prepared the design for the new Half Penny, One Penny, 2½d and Six Pence stamps.

114

After proofs from temporary and slightly differing copper plates had been studied by the King, the preparation of the various dies proceeded. For the bi-coloured stamps two dies were necessary, one for the head-plate (with small portrait) and one for the duty-plate, since these stamps were printed in two operations. Proofs from all the dies exist, some signed or initialled by Fuchs and marked as approved by the King. One of the Editors has a die proof of the One Penny signed by Herr Fuchs on June 25, 1901. Another has a die proof of the Half Penny initialled by Fuchs as approved on August 21, 1901, and a die proof of the small head signed by Fuchs as approved on July 27. This is marked on the back ' Appd by H.M.—A.E. 25/6/01 '.

Before passing from the question of design, it should be mentioned that in October 1902 essays known as ' Transvaal Essays ' were prepared with a view to improving the design of the stamps of the United Kingdom. As the name implies, these essays resembled closely the stamps prepared for the Transvaal. They are more handsome than any of the United Kingdom issues and exist in several different colours, both monocoloured and bi-coloured, but all of the value of ' 1d ', which appears in the two bottom corners of each stamp. There are two types of these essays. Type 2 has a wider white oval round the head than Type 1. It is believed that Type 2 exists only as a monocoloured stamp in green and in red. Perforated specimens of all these essays exist. (*See* Plates X and XI.)

The original issue of King Edward stamps was completed by values of Two Shillings & Six Pence, Five Shillings, Ten Shillings and One Pound, all of new design. Subsequently a monocoloured 4d was substituted for the bi-coloured stamp, and a new 7d stamp was added to the series.

Just prior to the King's death a new monocoloured 2d stamp was prepared, but this was not issued.

It was originally intended to include a Five Pounds stamp in the series, and a die was prepared of which proofs exist, but no plate was made from this. This die was registered in March 1902, and hardened on the 13th of that month.

PLATE X

1   A ' make-up ' prepared during the early days of the King's reign.   The surround of the head is taken from that used for the so-called ' Transvaal Essay ', but the black additions in both top corners were inserted by hand, and the value tablets were similarly altered.   The accepted ' Head ' die design has been cut out and the suggested one substituted.

2   Composite die proof of Head and Frame put together for the One Penny stamp issued January 1, 1902.   This proof bears the signature of the designer—Emil Fuchs—and the date of approval.

3   The approved make-up design for the $2\frac{1}{2}$d value.   The head is engraved and the frame is photographed.   This is mounted on a card marked ' B ' and ' July 10. 01 '.

4   Transvaal Essay.   Type 1.   Die proof of the Head of King Edward as adopted in reduced size for the stamps of his reign.

5   Transvaal Essay.   Type 2.   The white hair line which runs round the oval and joins the crown in Type 1 is deleted.

All the stamps concerned were manufactured by De La Rue until December 31, 1910, when their contract terminated, whereupon the work was undertaken either by Messrs Harrison & Sons Ltd, Printers in Ordinary to His Majesty the King, or by the Government printers at Somerset House, to whom respectively some of the De La Rue plates were handed over.

The machine-made paper was supplied by Messrs Turner & Co. Ltd, of Roughway Mills, near Tunbridge Wells. For all values up to One Shilling, and for the One Pound stamp, the watermark was the large Crown of 1880 (repeated three times on the One Pound stamp). The watermark of the Two Shillings & Six Pence, Five Shillings and Ten Shillings values was the large Anchor of the fiscal paper on which these were printed. The gum was colourless pure gum-arabic applied before printing. As will be mentioned later, a chalky surface was applied to the paper used for certain values at a later date, and in certain cases fluorescent inks were used.

The method of preparing the printing plates or electros was the electrotype process adopted by De La Rue for the surface-printed stamps since 1855, and the plates were surfaced with steel. In certain cases for monocoloured stamps De La Rue, and afterwards Harrison and Somerset House, printed from two plates (electros) simultaneously, the plates being placed side by side on the printing bed. If the two electros were made from the same forme they would be identical because the marginal lines, line-blocks, etc. were included as part of the forme. Each head- and duty-plate, and each plate used for the monocoloured stamps, can be identified by marks made by the printers in the marginal lines of rule, which appear usually in the bottom line towards the left of the sheet. In the case of bi-coloured stamps, great accuracy of register was necessary to ensure that the duty-plate impressions fell exactly where required on the sheets which had already received impressions from the head-plate.

Generally the plate consisted of 240 stamps in two panes, one above the other, each pane comprising 120 stamps in ten rows of twelve each.

The perforation of the De La Rue stamps was normally by horizontal comb machine gauging 14 to the space of 20 mm. The characteristic of this comb is that it always left a single extra perforation hole in every horizontal line of perforation on each side of the sheet. This is an almost infallible method of differentiating De La Rue stamps above the One Penny value up to the Ten Shillings stamp from those printed by Harrison and at Somerset House, because the latter were perforated by a vertical comb machine which provided no extra single perforation holes at the sides of the sheets. This distinction is specially useful for the monocoloured 4d, 7d, Five Shillings and Ten Shillings values, which are sometimes otherwise not easy to differentiate. There is, however, at least one instance of De La Rue using a vertical comb machine, namely, on some sheets of the 4d green and brown with continuous marginal green line, both on ordinary and chalk-surfaced paper. This variety is scarce.

For the One Pound stamp, which was three times the size of the other stamps with Crown watermark, a special horizontal comb machine was used not only by De La Rue but also at Somerset House. This provided a single extra perforation hole in each horizontal line on one side of the sheet only, the other side having the margin perforated throughout. The more usual method would seem to have been for the single extra perforation hole to be on the left of the sheet. Whether it appeared thus or on the right of the sheet would depend upon whether the sheet was fed into the machine from the top or the bottom.

The 14 gauge was maintained by Harrison and Somerset House when they took over the printing ; but Harrison soon changed the gauge to 15×14. A comb machine operating horizontally perforates the tops (or bottoms) and both sides of a row of stamps ; if operating vertically each operation perforates the top and bottom and one side of each stamp in a row. Inspection of the margins will show if the perforation was made horizontally or vertically, and whether the sheet was fed into the machine from the top or the bottom. Fluorescent ink is perceptible in some of the stamps of these issues, particulars of which are given later. This fluorescence, which shows as an unmistakable radiance under the quartz lamp, is due to the presence of eosin dye in the ink. The definition ' aniline ', commonly used to describe this phenomenon, is inaccurate because there are about a thousand aniline dyes.

It was originally intended to issue some of the new stamps on November 9, 1901, the King's birthday. The only plates available by then were those of the Half Penny and One Penny and it was not found possible to print in time the very large numbers required. So the issue was postponed until January 1, 1902, though a few copies of the Half Penny, One Penny, $2\frac{1}{2}$d and Six Pence (comprising the first issue) leaked out a little earlier.

Chapter Nineteen

Edward VII : Halfpenny

THIS value was issued on January 1, 1902, in deep bluish green. The Imprimatur Sheet was registered on September 26, 1901. The plate consisted of 240 stamps in two panes of 120 each, comprising ten rows of twelve. Between each pane there was a row of vertical lined blocks, four of such blocks occupying the space of one stamp. Each pane was surrounded by a continuous marginal line, rounded at the outer corners and square at the inner corners because the vertical lines ran continuously from pane to pane. The first Control Letter was A. This was placed below the eleventh stamp in the bottom row of the sheet. In December 1902 it was changed to B, still under the eleventh stamp. The bottom margin is found both imperforate and perforated. The Editors hesitated whether or not to refer to the perforation or otherwise of the margins, because this is of little, if any, philatelic interest. It depends simply upon whether, in the case of a horizontal comb machine, the top or the bottom of the sheet was fed in first; and in the case of a vertical comb machine, whether the sheet was fed into the machine from the left or the right side. However, since some of the Controls with perforated bottom margins are very scarce, and priced accordingly in the catalogue, mention of these will be made.

In December 1903 the Control Letter was changed to C, and this now appeared under the second stamp in the bottom row. This continued to be the position of the Controls for the remainder of the reign. In January 1904 the Control was changed to C4, and in April 1904 to D4. Controls C and C4 with perforated bottom margins are scarce and D4 thus is rare. The figure after the Control Letter denoted the year. The Control Letters and figures did not form part of the plate, but were attached thereto inside the printing frame. They could therefore be changed without modification of the plate itself.

Meanwhile in March 1902 sheets began to appear also with broken or co-extensive marginal lines. The first had Control B under the eleventh stamp. This is scarce and is only known with imperforate bottom margin. Similar sheets succeeded with Controls C (February 1903), C4 (January 1904) and D4 (April 1904) under the second stamp. C and C4 are unknown with perforated margin (although Stanley Gibbons's catalogue implies that they exist), and D4 is rare. Many cuts and marks of various descriptions appeared in the bottom lines of sheets of this stamp throughout its life from 1902 to 1911, denoting the use of a number of different plates. From these marks it is possible to identify at least sixty-four plates used by De La Rue, of which twenty had continuous lines of marginal rule. At least seven of the De La Rue plates were handed over to Harrison in 1911.

In November 1904 the colour of the stamp was changed to pale green or yellow green. The Imprimatur Sheet in the new colour was registered on July 15, 1904, and the issue was made on November 26, both from plates with continuous marginal lines and with co-extensive lines, with Control D4. With continuous marginal lines this Control is scarce, and is only known with imperforate margin, though Stanley Gibbons's catalogue implies that it exists perforated. With the co-extensive marginal lines the perforated margin variety is scarce. From this point printings were made only from plates with co-extensive marginal lines, and with Controls D5 (March 1905), E5 (September 1905), D6 (June 1906), F6 (August 1906), F7 (July 1907), G7 (September 1907), G8 (July 1908), H8 (October 1908), H9 (August 1909), I9 (November 1909), I10 (July 1910), and J10 (October 1910). On sheets with Control H9 the second stamp in the nineteenth row has the raised Crown watermark variety. D5 with perforated margin is scarce and E6 with perforated margin very rare.

Specimens with inverted watermark from sheets are very rare; but quite common from booklets, because 50 per cent of the latter had the watermark inverted. Only one full sheet with inverted watermark has been recorded. One sheet with

Control H9 had the two last stamps in the bottom row doubly printed, and portions of eleven more stamps in the two bottom rows partially so. There is also a constant variety showing a large white dot between the N and Y of HALFPENNY.

In March 1904 the One Penny stamp had appeared in booklet form. For this a special plate was required. This consisted of 240 stamps in four panes of 60 each in six vertical rows of ten, the first three vertical rows of each pane being inverted, and the third and fourth stamps of each row of six being *tête-bêche*. Twenty-four of these One Penny stamps were sold for two shillings and one halfpenny. In June 1906 Halfpenny stamps were included in the booklet, which consisted of twelve Penny and twenty-three Halfpenny stamps selling for two shillings. A special Halfpenny plate was made on which, in every fourth block of six stamps, one stamp was a dummy marked with a large X in green. The five stamps and dummy always appeared as the last sheet in the booklet. In August 1907 a further change was made, the booklets containing eighteen Penny stamps (in three blocks of six) and eleven Halfpenny stamps (in one block of six and one of five) still priced at two shillings. For this a new Half Penny plate was required, since the X for the dummy had to appear in every second block of stamps. The use of the dummy stamp was eventually discontinued.

In January 1911, Harrison took over the manufacture of the Halfpenny stamps, but specimens of their work did not appear until May 3 with Control A11. De La Rue plates with broken or co-extensive marginal lines were used, and the perforation remained 14. The work was inferior to that of De La Rue. The printing was blotchy or smudged, the register of the perforation was often faulty, the gum was more thinly applied and the range in colour was considerable, from dull green, through pale and medium yellowish green and bright green to deep green. A very vivid bright green shade, issued in August 1911 to a few Post Offices, is scarce. At least one sheet was perforated so badly that almost exact quarters of four stamps are comprised within the confines of a single perforation which is slightly diagonal. The A11 Control can be found in a large number of slightly different types with many sub-varieties. This is due to the fact that a number of different plates were used for these printings. The bottom margin was more often perforated than imperforate. The *British Philatelist* (Vol. X, No. 3) chronicled this stamp with watermark sideways, and it is listed thus in Stanley Gibbons's catalogue. The only copy of this variety known to the Editors is a used specimen in the Royal Collection postmarked August 26, 1911. This is a Harrison print perforated 14. It shows two portions of the Crown watermark. On one side is an almost complete Crown and on the other about 2 mm of the bottom of another Crown. It is difficult to conjecture how this variety occurred. If even half a sheet (to take a pane), were laid sideways on the plate, it would not fit because each pane had ten rows of twelve stamps, whereas the watermarks sideways would be in twelve rows of ten ; and if a whole sheet as printed were laid across the plate, in addition to the above phenomenon, only about half the plate would be covered by the paper. It is possible that this variety occurred on a booklet sheet.

On October 30, 1911, this stamp began to appear with perforation 15 × 14, the shades ranging from pale to deep and fairly bright green. There is an interesting variety showing an S.W. corner block of nine with Control A11 which is wholly imperforate, though the impression of the pins just shows on the surface of the paper, which, however, is not pierced by a single pin. The tenth stamp in the eighteenth row of one of the plates shows the frame lines on both sides of the stamp broken or damaged and partially repaired.

The 15 × 14 perforation is generally better registered than before. It is clear that different sets of pins were used because in some cases the diameter of the holes is about twice as large as in others ; and many different comb heads were used for this stamp.

Harrison also took over the De La Rue booklet plates, including the one (or more) with the dummy stamp consisting of a large X referred to above ; and they used this, although the principle of charging a halfpenny for the dummy had been discontinued. These booklet sheets were perforated 14, and specimens with the dummy printed by Harrison, which are easily distinguishable from the De La Rue prints, are scarce.

Chapter Twenty

Edward VII : One Penny

THIS stamp also was issued on January 1, 1902, in sheets of 240 in two panes separated by vertical line-blocks or pillars, as in the case of the Halfpenny. On completion of the plate in October 1901 colour trials were made in mauve on white paper, in two shades of mauve on red paper and in seven different shades of pink, red, carmine and lake on white paper. Imperforate gummed specimens of all of these are known with Crown watermark. Plate proofs are also known in green on thick card (including a double print), and in red on yellow paper with no watermark. Eventually a scarlet shade was selected, which differed from all the above-mentioned colour trials. Issued specimens were in more carmine shades, from pale to deep. There is also a rare carmine-vermilion or blood-red shade.

Imperforate Harrison plate proofs exist overprinted CAN-CELLED diagonally. The colour of these is true scarlet, and the ink is fluorescent, indicating a medium content of eosin dye. The Imprimatur Sheet was registered on October 14, 1901. The perforation was 14, and remarks concerning this in connection with the Halfpenny value apply equally to the One Penny Stamp. The marginal lines round the panes were continuous, rounded at the outer corners but square at the inner corners of the panes by the lined blocks. The first Control Letter was A. In every case the Control appeared under the eleventh stamp in the bottom row. Succeeding Controls with continuous marginal lines were B (December 1902), C (December 1903), C4 (February 1904), D4 (April 1904) and D5 (July 1905). The last is scarce ; and the others (except A) are scarce with perforated bottom margin. D5 with perforated margin is unknown to the Editors, but Stanley Gibbons's catalogue indicates that it exists.

At the end of 1903 sheets with co-extensive marginal lines began to appear, the first with Control C (December 1903), succeeded by C4 (February 1904), D4 (April 1904), D5 (June 1905), E5 (August 1905), E6 (July 1906), F6 (September 1906), F7 (July 1907), G7 (October 1907), G8 (July 1908), H8 (October 1908), H9 (July 1909), I9 (October 1909), I10 (July 1910) and J10 (September 1910). C, C4, D4, D5 and E6 are rare with perforated bottom margin. As in the case of the Halfpenny, there are numerous cuts and marks in various positions along the bottom marginal lines. From these it is possible to identify at least seventy plates used by De La Rue, of which twenty had continuous lines of marginal rule. At least six of the De La Rue plates were handed over to Harrison in 1911. On some sheets with Controls I9, I10 and J10 there is a flaw under the E of PENNY on the tenth stamp in the bottom row ; and on another stamp the oval to the left of the King's head is broken. On sheets with Controls H9 and I9, the second stamp in the nineteenth row has the raised Crown watermark variety. The stamps for booklets have already been described in connection with the Halfpenny value. The first of the special plates for booklet printing was registered on September 18, 1903. Copies of the One Penny used from Ascension in November 1911 have a very rare cancellation, showing the index letter ' C ' of the cancellation sideways. Only five of these have been recorded.

Harrison took over the manufacture of these stamps in January 1911. Their printings appeared first on or about May 3, 1911. They all had co-extensive marginal lines. The Control was A11 and perforation 14. With this perforation the normal Control was wide, i.e. the distance between the figures of ' 11 ' was $1\frac{1}{2}$ mm; but rarely the narrow Control is found with perforation 14. In this case the distance between the figures of ' 11 ' is only 1 mm. Only the narrow Control appears with stamps perforated 15×14 which appeared on October 6, 1911. Stanley Gibbons's catalogue lists (unpriced) the Harrison One Penny imperforate. The Editors have no record of its having been issued thus to the public ; but imperforate proofs on paper with normal watermark and gum are believed to exist.

The shades of the Harrison printings were numerous, in two main groups, namely rose-red and rose-carmine. There are also shades of deep bright scarlet and the so-called ' aniline pink', perforated 14. This is quite different from any of the normal shades and is really pale pink or pale rosine. Copies also exist in ' aniline rose '. Both these varieties are strongly fluorescent under the quartz lamp. There is a rare variety in deep dull red on thick rough mottled paper with no watermark. At least one sheet was perforated so badly that the vertical perforation almost bisects many of the stamps.

Generally the Harrison stamps can be distinguished by blotchiness or smudginess, bad alignment of perforation, inadequate gum and considerable variation in shade, as compared with the productions of De La Rue. One sheet perforated 14 is recorded as having been issued without gum. Perforation with large or small holes, referred to in connection with the Halfpenny, applies also to the One Penny values, and many different comb heads were also used for the perforation of this stamp.

Specimen booklets exist containing eighteen One Penny stamps in three blocks, and blocks of six and five of the Halfpenny with dummy added, all cancelled with a special double ring stamp of ' London Chief Office E.C. ' These were issued with announcements that stamps of the new reign (George V) would be issued in June 1911 without the X dummy. As in the case of the Halfpenny, numerous varieties of the A11 Control, both wide and narrow, exist.

Chapter Twenty One

Edward VII : Threehalfpence

APART from the addition of a Crown and the substitution of the small Fuchs head of the King on the head-plate, this stamp resembled its Victorian predecessor in design and colours. The plate consisted of 240 stamps in the usual two panes, which were separated by a row of plain paper the depth of a stamp. The Imprimatur Sheet was registered on February 1, 1902, and the stamp issued on March 21. The paper and gum were normal for the issues of De La Rue, and the perforation was 14 by horizontal comb, leaving a single extra perforation hole at each side of the sheet. The colours were dull to deep purple and shades of bright green.

Eighteen different colour trials are known, all monocoloured. Nine of these are on white and nine on coloured paper.

De La Rue made eight head- and four duty-plates. They used six head- and three duty-plates, and handed over to Somerset House in 1911, two head-plates already used and two unused ; also one used and one unused duty-plate. All these can be identified and differentiated by marginal marks.

The First Setting had the purple marginal line continuous all round the panes, rounded at the outer corners but square at the inner corners of the panes ; with continuous green lines at the sides only of the panes. This setting is rare.

The Second Setting (which also appeared in 1902) was the same as the first, except that the continuous purple lines were rounded (instead of square) at the inner corners of the panes. There were continuous green lines at the sides of the panes.

The Third Setting (1904) had both the purple and green lines continuous all round the panes and rounded at the corners. There were small breaks in the green lines at the N.W. corners of both panes and at the S.W. corner of the upper pane.

This stamp appeared on chalk-surfaced paper early in September 1905 in shades varying from very deep to pale dull

purple, and green varying from pale yellowish to deep bright
bluish.   There was a block of twelve in the Crawford collection
in very pale purple and bright green marked 'No watermark'.
Some of the watermarks are not visible, but this is no doubt
due to special thickness of the paper and the heavy coating of
chalk surface.

The First Setting on the chalk-surfaced paper was the same
as for the Third Setting on the ordinary paper, namely, purple
and green lines continuous all round the panes.

The Second Setting on chalky paper had continuous purple
lines round the panes and green lines at the sides only.

The Third Setting on chalky paper had co-extensive purple lines
all round the panes, with continuous green lines at the sides only.

The Fourth Setting on chalky paper had co-extensive purple
lines all round the panes and the inner corners of the panes were
characterized by square purple dots, this being the only case in
which this head-plate was used by De La Rue.   The green lines
were at the sides only.

The Fifth Setting on chalky paper had co-extensive purple
lines, and green lines continuous all round the panes.

When the marginal lines are described as continuous all round
the panes, this is not strictly accurate because certain breaks or
cuts appear.

The Somerset House printings were as follows :

The First Series of Printings appeared on July 13, 1911, on
ordinary unsurfaced paper in reddish-purple and deep bright
green.   There were co-extensive purple lines, and continuous
green lines, all round the panes.   The purple corner pieces at
the inner corners of the panes were square.   A V cut was added
under the fifth stamp in the purple line below the lower pane ;
there were normal breaks under the sixth and seventh stamps ;
and broad ' | | ' cuts under the eleventh stamp in the bottom row
of the lower pane.   There was no coloured dot above the last
stamp in the top row or below the last stamp in the bottom
row of either pane.   The First Series of Printings was small and
marginal corner blocks are rare.

9

The Second Series of Printings appeared on September 29, 1911, and was similar to the First Series except that there were narrow ' | | ' cuts in the purple line below the eleventh stamp in the bottom row of the lower pane, with a small purple dot above the last stamp in the top row and below the last stamp in the bottom row of each pane ; a single cut in the purple line below the eighth stamp in the bottom row of the sheet ; and no V cut under the fifth stamp. The corner pieces at the inner corners of the panes were square. The purple ranged in shade from pale reddish to dull greyish and very deep. The green was bright bluish. The head-plate used for this series had not been used by De La Rue.

The Third Series of Printings appeared from February to April, 1912. Both the purple and green lines were co-extensive and there were ' | | ' cuts in the purple line under the last stamp in the bottom row of the lower pane to the left of the ' 1 ' of ' 1½d '. Although these are always in the same position, they vary considerably in aspect during the course of a long series of printings, sometimes showing white dots on either side of, and sometimes between, the cuts. In some cases also traces of the filled-up cuts under the eleventh stamp are apparent. The corner pieces at the inner corners of the panes were square. Between February and April 1912 the marginal lines and cuts were cleaned up. Those under the last stamp became clear and sharp and all traces of those under the eleventh stamp disappeared. There was a purple dot above the last stamp in the top row and below the last stamp in the bottom row of each pane. The purple varied in shade from deep dark to greyish or slate, and eventually to deep reddish. Some of the printings of the Third Series were in fluorescent purple ink.

The Fourth Series of Printings (probably May 1912) was marked by ' | | ' cuts in the purple line under the last stamp in the bottom row of the lower pane, under, but to the left of, the figure ' 1 ' of ' 1½d ', i.e. considerably more to the right than for the Third Series. A purple dot still appeared above the last stamp in the top row and below the last stamp in the bottom row

of each pane. The purple corner pieces of the inner corners
of the panes were square. The shades were deep reddish purple
and deep green. Most of the printings of this Series were in
fluorescent purple ink.

The Fifth and last Series of Printings appeared late in October
1912, contemporaneously with the issue of the George V stamps.
The setting was similar to that of the Fourth Series, except that
the ' | | ' cuts in the purple line under the last stamp in the bottom
row of the lower pane were narrower and slightly more to the
right. The shades were reddish-purple, and green ranging from
pale bright to deep. The purple ink used for this Series was
not fluorescent. There were no date cuts in the marginal lines
of the upper panes of any of the Somerset House printings of
the 1½d.

Chapter Twenty Two

Edward VII : Twopence

APART from the incorporation of the small Fuchs head and a Crown in the head-plate, the design and colouring of this value were similar to those of its Victorian predecessor. The paper, watermark, perforation and gum were also similar ; and the sheet again consisted of 240 stamps in two panes, with a blank row of paper between the panes. The Imprimatur Sheet was registered on March 15, 1902. The colours were pale yellow-green and carmine. It was issued on March 25, 1902. Sixteen different colour trials are known. These are all monocoloured. Nine are on white and seven on coloured paper. De La Rue made six head- and three duty-plates, and used five head- and two duty-plates. They handed over to Somerset House two head-plates (one unused) and one used and one unused duty-plate.

The First Setting had a continuous green line all round the panes with short carmine bars at the top and bottom, and at the sides, of each pane opposite the value tablets.

The Second Setting (early 1903) was altered slightly by making the corners of the green lines more rounded, and the colour was bluish- or greyish-green. On some of the stamps of this issue the carmine ink shows a blood-red flash-up under the quartz lamp.

The First Setting on chalky paper. On September 6, 1905, the stamps appeared on chalk-surfaced paper. The state of the marginal lines was the same as before, but in many cases the carmine bars were hardly perceptible, and in some cases non-existent. The colours were deep greyish-green and deep carmine, which shows a blood-red flash-up under the lamp.

The Second Setting on chalky paper (1910) had co-extensive green lines rounded at all four corners of the panes ; and carmine bars as before.

Early in 1910 a monocoloured stamp was prepared known as the 2d ' Tyrean plum '. Several colour trials of this are

known ; also two essays which were rejected by the King when
he approved the design adopted. These essays are similar to
the adopted design, an Imprimatur Sheet of which was registered
on April 11, 1910, and a number of sheets were printed. A
complete perforated sheet (less one copy) was shown by the
General Post Office at the London International Stamp Exhibi-
tion at Grosvenor House in 1950. Owing to the King's death on
May 6, 1910, the whole stock was destroyed with the exception of
the sheet above referred to, and a very few other copies, one of which
went through the post to the Prince of Wales, afterwards King
George V, in whose collection there is also an unused pair. Die
proofs in various colours exist, and some perforated copies overprinted SPECIMEN. Without the overprint, copies are of extreme
rarity. Owing to the decision not to issue the monocoloured
stamp, there was an unexpected demand for the bi-coloured
stamp, and two more issues of this were made on chalky paper,
one with continuous and one with co-extensive green lines, in
deep dull green and greyish green respectively.

The First Series of Printings at Somerset House appeared
on August 8, 1911, on ordinary paper. The green lines were
co-extensive and the carmine bars very rudimentary. At first
there were no green dots above the last stamp in the top row or
below the last stamp in the bottom row of either pane ; but these
were soon added. There were ' | | ' cuts in the green line below
the eleventh stamp in the bottom row of the lower pane. The
colours were pale to deep grey-green and carmine. Included
in this printing was what is known as the ' Lozenge ' variety.
It consists of a distorted value tablet, the right side of the
tablet being abnormally short and the curved side above much
elongated. This variety has also been recorded as printed by
De La Rue on chalky paper.

The Second Series of Somerset House Printings (November 22,
1911) was similar to the first except that a diagonal cut was
added in the green line under the eleventh stamp in the bottom
row of both panes. Exceptionally some of the deeper shades of
carmine of this series are fluorescent. Specimens of this are rare.

The Third Series of Somerset House Printings (March 11, 1912) was from a previously unused head-plate and a previously unused duty plate, both the green and carmine marginal lines being co-extensive. Two white dots (instead of cuts) appeared in the green line below the last stamp in the bottom row of the lower pane. The colours were deep grey-green and carmine. The carmine ink of this series is fluorescent. One of the Editors has a copy of this stamp bisected diagonally and used on piece with date stamp ' Codford St Mary January 26, 1912 '. As such use was illegal the cancellation may have been applied by mistake or complacency.

Chapter Twenty Three

Edward VII : Twopence Halfpenny

THE design was similar to that of the Halfpenny and One Penny, with the larger King's head in an oval ; but in this case the value was shown in figures at the bottom of the stamp. The Imprimatur Sheet was registered on December 3, 1901. There exists a series of eight very rare essays, each showing differences in the lower portion of the stamp. In addition to the usual die proofs, there were also nine colour trials on paper with normal watermark, perforation and gum. These were in varying shades of blue. It was originally intended to print this stamp in mauve on blue paper, and the Imprimatur Sheet was registered thus, and two thousand sheets were so printed, copies from which exist. It was, however, finally decided that the issue should be in bright blue on white paper, and the plate was re-registered thus on December 17, 1901. The official issue was on January 1, 1902. The sheet consisted of 240 stamps in two panes, with a row of vertical line-blocks or pillars between the panes. The paper, watermark, perforation and gum were the same as for the other printings by De La Rue on ordinary unsurfaced paper. The colour of the issue ranged from rather pale blue to bright blue and deep blue.

Originally the blue marginal lines were continuous all round the panes, and the vertical side lines ran across the gaps between the panes so as to include the pillars. From about 1903 the marginal lines were co-extensive. De La Rue made eight plates, five with continuous marginal rule and three with co-extensive lines. They used only seven of these, and handed over to Harrison seven of these, including the one which had not been used.

Harrison took over the manufacture in 1911, and specimens of their work first appeared on July 10, 1911. The marginal lines were co-extensive ; but on September 29, 1911, specimens appeared from plates with continuous lines.

PLATE XI

1 The original 3d Victoria design.

2 Essay made up from the framework of the Queen Victoria stamp with the centre cut out and a lithographed head design of King Edward inserted.

3 The original design was altered. The crown and lower leaves were drawn by hand and superimposed.

4 These alterations adopted for the issued design.

5 to 12

Eight essays prepared by De La Rue for the $2\frac{1}{2}$ pence stamp of 1901.

PLATE XI

The Harrison prints were dull and rather blotchy as compared with the De La Rue work, and the perforation is usually less well registered. It was by vertical comb. Specimens exist with watermark inverted. These are scarce.

On October 4, 1911, the gauge of the perforation was changed to 15 × 14. There are marked shades with this perforation, ranging from pale dull blue to deep bright blue, and the gum varies considerably from dull colourless to yellow shiny. The following minor varieties are known :

(a) The word REVENUE appears to read REVENOE, owing to damage to, or clogging of, the letter ' U ' on one stamp ;

(b) The lower pane of one of the plates shows certain damage to the right frame lines of some of the stamps in the right-hand vertical row of the pane.

Chapter Twenty Four

Edward VII : Threepence

APART from the substitution of the King's head and the incorporation of a Crown in the design, the 3d stamp resembled its Victorian predecessor, except that the side leaves below the value were redrawn. It was the only stamp of the Edward VII series printed on coloured paper. The Imprimatur Sheet was registered on February 1, 1902, and the date of issue was March 20. The sheet, as usual, comprised 240 stamps in two panes, which were separated by a line of pillars. There was a continuous purple marginal line around the panes, and this extended across the space between the panes. The ink was purple, but appeared as brown on the yellow paper. The purple varied from medium almost to black ; and the yellow of the paper from lemon to chrome. The perforation was 14 by means of the usual horizontal comb machine.

On March 31, 1906, appeared the first issue on chalk-surfaced paper, which was yellow-orange at first ; then lemon-yellow and finally pale orange. The purple varied from very pale to very deep. There were two varieties of the orange paper, one showing orange back and front, and the other showing it only on the front. De La Rue made five plates, four of which they used for printings both on the ordinary and chalky papers. They handed over three plates to Harrison, including one unused. Harrison used only one plate for the stamps, perforated 14, and three plates for those with compound perforation.

The first specimens printed by Harrison appeared on September 14, 1911. The perforation was 14 by means of a vertical comb machine. The paper was ordinary unsurfaced and there was no change in the setting. The Harrison prints were blotchy, the perforation less regular and the gum less thick than before. The purple resembled chocolate on the pale yellow paper. The issue perforated 14 is scarce because it was made to only a few

Post Offices over a period of about a fortnight. The 15 × 14 perforation was first noticed on September 25, 1911. The purple was generally very dark, but sometimes greyish, and the paper was canary or bright lemon. A rare variety perforated 15 × 14 is recorded in grey on lemon paper. The following minor varieties are known with both perforations :

(a) In one of the plates, on the last stamp in the ninth row of the upper pane, the outer line of the frame of the design is missing in two places on the right side ;

(b) The same stamp, as above, but showing obvious repairs ;

(c) In another of the plates, on the last stamp in the eighth row of the upper pane, the outer frame line of the stamp above the value tablet is bulged outwards.

Chapter Twenty Five

Edward VII : Fourpence

THE bi-coloured 4d resembled its Victorian predecessor except for the change to the King's head, the addition of a Crown to the head-plate, the addition of small ornaments in the centre at each side, and the one at the bottom was reversed in shape as compared with the Victorian stamp. In this case the spaces between the stamps, and between the stamps and the brown marginal lines, were filled with fine lines of shading which were bisected by the perforation. Twenty-one separate colour trials are known. These are all monocoloured. Thirteen are on white and eight on coloured paper. The make-up of the sheets differed from the Victorian make-up, which consisted of 320 stamps in 16 panes of 20 each ; but normally issued only in sheets of 4 panes each. For the Edward stamps the sheets consisted of the usual 240 stamps in two panes one above the other. The row between the two panes was left blank.

The Imprimatur Sheet was registered on March 29, 1902, three days *after* the issue to the public on March 26.

Some of the sheets of these stamps, both on ordinary and chalk-surfaced paper, were perforated with a vertical comb instead of the normal horizontal comb, but this variety is rare.

De La Rue made and used six head-plates and two duty-plates. Four of the head-plates had continuous lines of marginal rule, with certain breadths, and two had co-extensive lines. The two duty-plates had continuous lines. On the ordinary paper the colours were dull green and shades of brown, grey-brown, chocolate-brown, and red brown.

The First Setting had the green lines continuous all round the panes, but with all the corners cut away except the S.E. corner of the upper pane. In a second state this corner also was cut away. Three head-plates and one duty-plate were used for this setting on ordinary paper.

The printings on chalk-surfaced paper appeared on January 19, 1906. These at first had both the brown and green lines continuous all round the panes, i.e. with no breaks at the corners, but the corners of the green lines were soon cut away. The brown of these printings varied from dull palish to very deep or bright reddish. The green varied from olive to deep green. Later printings of this stamp on chalk-surfaced paper had the continuous brown line as before, but the green lines were co-extensive. The shades were deep bright chocolate-brown and fairly deep green. On the chalk-surfaced paper specimens are not uncommon in which the shading is wholly or partially missing from the interior of one or more of the figures ' 4 '. Sometimes also portions of the shading are missing from the circles of the value tablets.

The monocoloured 4d stamp in orange appeared on November 1, 1909, the Imprimatur Sheet having been registered on October 21. The stamp was similar in design to its predecessor, but of course from a new single die, which differed in many small details from the bi-coloured stamps. The make-up of the sheet was the same as before, but the space between the panes was filled with vertical lined blocks. Thin co-extensive lines surrounded both panes, and at each corner there were short vertical and horizontal connecting lines, varying at the different corners. The paper was ordinary unsurfaced. The first issue was in brown orange, followed by shades of pale yellow-orange and bright orange. The perforation was, as usual, by horizontal comb. De La Rue made and used four plates, three of which they handed over to Harrison.

Printings by Harrison with perforation 14 by a vertical comb machine were first noticed on July 13, 1911. They are sometimes not easy to distinguish from the De La Rue printings, but generally speaking the Harrison stamps are slightly paler, less clearly defined and less accurately perforated. The gum is quite colourless and thin and, if side marginal copies are available, the lack of the extra perforation hole in the side margins identifies the Harrison stamps. Stamps perforated 15 × 14 appeared on November 6, 1911. The shades of the Harrison prints were bright and reddish-orange.

Chapter Twenty Six

Edward VII: Fivepence

THIS value again was similar to its Victorian predecessor except for the change of head, the addition of a Crown in the head-plate, re-drawing of the ornaments on each side at the top and the V-shaped ornaments on the tops of the value tablets replaced by dots. The make-up of the sheets was the same as before, namely 240 stamps in two panes, with a row of blank paper between the panes. The Imprimatur Sheet was registered on May 3, 1902, and the issue made on May 14. Owing to the incorporation of a Crown in the head-plate, the figures of value came lower on the stamps. Consequently the position of the duty-plate in relation to the head-plate had to be lowered; and throughout the issues of this stamp it will be found that at the tops of the panes the blue marginal lines are superimposed on the purple ones; and that at the bottom of each pane the blue lines are about one-eighth of an inch below the purple lines. The early shades were dull purple and bright blue.

De La Rue made five head-plates and four duty-plates, and used all of them except one head-plate. They handed over to Somerset House two head-plates, one of which had not been used, and one duty-plate.

The only setting for the De La Rue stamps on ordinary paper consisted of continuous purple lines round the panes, and short blue bars at the top and bottom and at the sides of the panes more or less corresponding with the positions of the value tablets, though the vertical bars at the sides varied in length. The chalk-surfaced stamps appeared on May 19, 1906, with the same setting as before.

At some later date a new setting appeared with co-extensive purple lines, rounded at the outer corners of the panes and with square dots at the inner corners; with short blue bars as before. This setting with co-extensive purple lines is very rare.

In 1910 the setting was changed, showing both the purple and blue lines continuous all round the panes, with rounded unbroken corners. The colours were shades of dull purple and bright blue. The perforation of all the De La Rue stamps was by horizontal comb. There is a rare variety on the chalky paper with watermark inverted.

The First Series of Somerset House Printings appeared on August 7, 1911. The purple was deeper than before and the blue bright, ranging from pale to deep. Both purple and blue lines were continuous all round the panes. There were ' | | ' cuts in the purple line under the eleventh stamp in the bottom row of the lower pane. Purple dots appeared above the last stamp in the top row of each pane and below the last stamp in the bottom row of each pane.

The Second Series of Somerset House Printings (February 11, 1912) had co-extensive purple lines with rounded pieces at the outer corners of the panes and square dots at the inner corners ; and continuous blue lines all round the panes. There were ' | | ' cuts in the purple line under the eleventh stamp in the bottom rows of both panes, the cuts in the upper pane being below the lions, and in the lower pane below the harp.

The Third Series of Somerset House Printings (April 1912) had marginal lines as before, but with ' | | ' cuts in the purple line under the twelfth stamp in the bottom row of the lower pane only. In this series of printings the eleventh stamp in the bottom row of the sheet often shows the ' broken harp string ' variety, i.e. the first and sometimes the second string of the harp on the shield is broken. The shades were reddish-purple or dull purple and deep blue. The purple of some of the printings of this series is fluorescent.

The Fourth Series of Somerset House Printings (February 1913) was the same as before, except that there was no purple dot above the last stamp in the top row of either pane or below the last stamp in the bottom row of either pane. In this series there sometimes appeared the variety of the ' lion minus head ' on the last stamp in the bottom row of the lower pane. The second lion in the N.W. corner of the shield sometimes has no head. There is another variety which shows defects and distortion on the right-hand side of the arms shield alongside the backs of the lions in the S.E. corner of the shield ; also the horizontal line between the upper and lower portions of the shield is broken towards the end on the right, and the tail of the top lion of the three is non-existent for a considerable distance. This variety appears to be constant, but its position on the sheet is not known. The shades were dull and greyish-purple and pale blue.

The Fifth Series of Somerset House Printings (March 1913) was the same as the Fourth Series, except that a white dot appeared in the vertical purple line to the right of the last stamp in the bottom row of the lower pane ; and the paper is more highly glazed.

Chapter Twenty Seven

Edward VII: Sixpence

THE design of this was similar to that of the Halfpenny and One Penny with the large Fuchs head. The Imprimatur Sheet was registered on December 3, 1901, and issue made to the public on January 1, 1902. It is believed that at least four separate monocoloured colour trials exist. As usual, the sheet consisted of 240 stamps in two panes, with a row of vertical lined blocks or pillars between the panes. The perforation was 14 by means of a horizontal comb machine. De La Rue made eleven plates. Six of these had continuous marginal lines, and five had co-extensive lines. They used five plates with continuous lines for the printings on ordinary paper; and six plates with continuous lines, and three plates with co-extensive lines, for the printings on chalk-surfaced paper. They handed over to Somerset House one plate with continuous lines and five plates with co-extensive lines, of which two had not previously been used. Two plates, side by side, were printed from simultaneously. Until September 1905 the paper was ordinary unsurfaced. The shades ranged from quite deep dull purple to pale lilac.

Specimens on chalk-surfaced paper were first noted on October 1, 1905. The first printings on this paper had continuous marginal lines, as before. These were followed by prints from plates with co-extensive lines. The shades on chalky paper range from pale lilac through dull purple to deep bright purple.

The perforation was 14 by means of a vertical comb machine.

The distinguishing marks and characteristics of the Six Plates used for the Nine Series of Printings at Somerset House are given later. It should be noted that numbers given to the plates are Somerset House numberings, and do not correspond with the sequence of the eleven plates made by De La Rue.

10

First Series of Somerset House Printings : October to November 1911 : Plates 1 and 2

Plate 1. ' | | ' cuts under the EN of PENCE below the eleventh stamp in the bottom row of the lower pane ; two scoops, containing dots, out of the last pillar only between the panes ; a coloured dot under the last stamp in the bottom row and above the last stamp in the top row of the sheet ; a single cut under the letter X of SIXPENCE below the first stamp in the bottom row of the lower pane ; marginal lines co-extensive ; a coloured dot in the centre of the left margin beside the lined blocks. Plate 1 was used only for the First Series of printings.

Plate 2. ' | | ' cuts parallel under the CE of PENCE below the eleventh stamp in the bottom row of the lower pane ; scoops containing dots, out of the last two pillars between the panes ; a coloured dot under the last stamp in the bottom row and above the last stamp in the top row of the sheet ; single cuts under the second and fourth stamps in the bottom row of the lower pane ; a coloured dot in the right margin beside the pillars. The break in the line under the seventh stamp in the bottom row is smaller than that under the sixth, and similar breaks reversed appeared above the sixth and seventh stamps in the top row of the sheet. Plate 2 was used also for the Second and Third Series of printings, and for part of the Fourth Series.

A few sheets from both plates were first printed in what was described as 'magenta' or bright plum or Royal purple on chalk-surfaced paper. Apparently the colour produced on this paper was not considered satisfactory and attempts were made to prevent any of these stamps getting out, though the colour was bright and pleasing. Nearly all the sheets were destroyed, but a few specimens survived, including copies from the bottom row showing date cuts. Two complete bottom rows (one since broken up), a block, a pair and a single, all with date cuts, from Plate 2 have been recorded, and Charles Nissen had a pair with date cuts from Plate 1. Over thirty years ago one of the Editors saw specimens of this rarity, not including copies from the bottom ow with cuts, at the General Post Office, and an Imprimatur heet in ' magenta ' on chalky paper was registered.

Although the First Series of printings all appeared within period of one month, the colours and shades are very numerous nd the differences quite extraordinary.   Apparently the printers t Somerset House experienced difficulty in achieving uniformity, nd the various colours tried may have been to some extent xperimental.   As Plates 1 and 2 were printed from simultane- usly, the same colours and shades appeared from both plates. he colours, with dates of their appearance, were as follows : 3right plum, violet or Royal purple (October 31, 1911) ; dull lum and deep plum (November 9 to 16, 1911) ; deep mauve and eep plum (November 28, 1911).   All the printings of the First eries were in fluorescent ink.

econd Series of Somerset House Printings : March to April 1912 :
   Plates 2 and 3

Plate 2.   ' | | ' cuts removed from below the eleventh stamp in he bottom row of the sheet, and very fine ' | | ' cuts added under he EN of PENCE below the twelfth stamp in the bottom row f the lower pane.   These cuts soon wore away or became filled p, and they can be found with three distinct varieties, namely, lear, obscure, and practically non-existent. The dot in the ight margin beside the pillars was removed, and the single cut nder the fourth stamp in the bottom row of the sheet was filled p.   Otherwise the state of this Plate was the same as for the First Series of printings.   This state of Plate 2 is scarce.

Plate 3.   This had co-extensive marginal lines, but the bottom eft-hand corner piece in the sheet was joined to the left-hand vertical marginal line.   There were parallel ' || ' cuts under the E of PENCE below the twelfth stamp in the bottom row of the sheet, and a single cut under the first stamp ; there were scoops, containing dots, out of the last pillar only between the panes (differing slightly from those on Plate 1).   There was a coloured lot below the last stamp in the bottom row of the sheet and above she last stamp in the top row.   The breaks under the sixth and seventh stamps in the bottom row were approximately equal i size. Plate 3 was used also for the Third, Fourth, Fifth, Eightl and Ninth Series of printings.

For the Second Series of printings the colours were shade of dull purple and lilac, and all the printings were in fluorescen ink.

Third Series of Somerset House Printings : May 1912 : Plates and 3

Plate 2. The ' | | ' cuts were renewed under the loop of the of PENCE below the last stamp in the bottom row; these wer fairly thick and from 1 to 1½ mm wide ; a white dot was adde in the vertical line to the right of the last stamp in the botton row ; traces of the old cuts under the eleventh stamp often showe and there is a well-known variety showing the cuts under botl the eleventh and twelfth stamps. This was caused by th stoppings of the cuts under the eleventh stamp having faller out. They were soon replaced and this variety is rare.

Plate 3. The state of this was the same as for the Secon Series of printings, except that a white dot was added in th vertical marginal line to the right of the last stamp in the botton row.

During the Third Series of printings the plates were re surfaced or repaired, which caused slight variations in the cuts dots, etc. The shades were deep and dull purple. The ink fo this series was not fluorescent.

Fourth Series of Somerset House Printings : June 1912 : Plates to a limited extent), 3 and 4

Plate 2. The state was the same as for the Third Serie of printings, except that the white dot in the right-hand vertica marginal line was removed from the twentieth to the nineteentl row of the sheet, and all traces of the ' || ' cuts under the eleventl stamp were removed. Plate 2 was used only for a short time, and then discarded for good and replaced by Plate 4, for this serie of printings.

Plate 3 was in the same state as for the Third Series of printings, except that the white dot in the right-hand vertical marginal line was removed from the end of the twentieth to the end of the nineteenth row.

Plate 4. This had continuous lines all round the panes, fairly broad ' | | ' cuts under the E of PENCE below the last stamp in the bottom row of the sheet, and a single cut under the second stamp. There was a white dot in the vertical marginal line to the right of the nineteenth row ; there were scoops, containing dots, out of the last two pillars for the upper dot, and out of the penultimate pillar only for the lower dot ; there was a coloured dot under the last stamp of the bottom row and above the last stamp in the top row of the sheet. Plate 4 was used only for part of the Fourth Series of printings and for the Fifth Series.

The colour of the Fourth Series of printings was shades of deep purple and greyish-purple. A considerable portion of this Series was printed in ink which fluoresces to a greater or lesser extent. This was the last Series of printings of this stamp for which fluorescent ink was used.

Fifth Series of Somerset House Printings : October 1912 : Plates 3 and 4

Plate 3 was in the same state as for the Fourth Series of printings, except that the coloured dots were removed from above the last stamp in the top row of the sheet and from below the last stamp in the bottom row ; the dots were removed from the scoops in the pillars between the panes ; and the white dot in the vertical line on the right of the lower pane was removed from the end of the nineteenth to the end of the eighteenth row.

Plate 4 was in the same state as for the Fourth Series of printings except that the coloured dots were removed from above the last stamp in the top row of the sheet and from below the last stamp in the bottom row ; the dots were removed from the scoops in the pillars between the panes ; and the white dot in the

vertical line on the right of the lower pane was removed from
the end of the nineteenth to the end of the eighteenth row. The
last stamp in the top row of the lower pane was damaged, the
right frame line having a broad white line extending from the
middle of the oak leaves to the bottom of the stamp. The last
stamp in the second row from the bottom of the sheet had the
outer frame line cracked.

The colour of the Fifth Series of printings was shades of
reddish-purple and dull purple.

Sixth Series of Somerset House Printings : November 1912 Plates 5 and 6

Plate 5 had fine ' | | ' cuts, barely 1 mm broad, under the loop
of the P of PENCE below the last stamp in the bottom row of the
lower pane. There were no coloured dots above the last stamp
in the top row of the sheet or below the last stamp in the bottom
row ; there were no scoops out of the pillars between the panes ;
the vertical marginal line to the right of the lined blocks was
comparatively thick ; there were slight traces of breaks in the
bottom marginal line below the sixth and seventh stamps, but
differing slightly from those on Plate 6 ; there was a white dot
in the vertical marginal line to the right of the last stamp in the
eighteenth row of the sheet. This was to the left of the marginal
line, instead of in the centre.

Plate 6 was similar to Plate 5 except that the ' | | ' cuts below
the last stamp in the bottom row were more to the left and under
the serif at the foot of the P of PENCE ; there was a white dot
in the vertical line to the right of the eighteenth row ; this was
in the middle, instead of to the left of the line, as in the case of
Plate 5. The vertical line to the right of the pillars between the
panes was comparatively thin ; and the S.W. corner piece of
the lower pane, and nearly all the left side co-extensive lines, were
dropped slightly below the normal level, i.e. the level of the stamps.
The colour of the Sixth Series of printings was shades of reddish

or greyish-purple, deep to pale. Plates 5 and 6 had not been previously used by De La Rue.

Seventh Series of Somerset House Printings : March to April 1913 : Plates 5 and 6

(*a*) The first printing of this Series was on paper experimentally surfaced with something resembling chalk, and which had white opaque gum.

Plate 5. The state was exactly the same as for the Sixth Series.

Plate 6. The state was exactly the same as for the Sixth Series.

The colour was shades of dull plum, pale purple and rosy lilac.

(*b*) The experimentally-surfaced paper was soon discarded and printings were resumed on ordinary unsurfaced paper similar to that of the Sixth Series.

Plate 5. The state was exactly the same as for the Sixth Series.

Plate 6. The state was exactly the same as for the Sixth Series.

It is sometimes difficult to distinguish between the printings from the Sixth Series and those from the Seventh Series on ordinary paper ; but in the Seventh Series the tones and shades were generally paler and the paper more highly glazed.

Eighth Series of Somerset House Printings : June 1913 : Plates 3 and 5

Plate 3. The marginal state was the same as for the Fifth Series of printings from this plate, except that the single cut under the first stamp in the bottom row was filled up.

Plate 5. The marginal state was the same as for the Sixth and Seventh Series of printings from this plate.

The shades were paler and the paper thinner and more highly glazed than for the previous printings.

Ninth Series of Somerset House Printings : July 1913 : Plates 3 and 5

This series was printed on thick paper heavily coated with chalk. The gum was yellow and often streaky, and the colour was slight shades of deep bright purple.

Plate 3. The marginal state was the same as for the Eighth Series, but a vertical crack in the vertical line to the right of the pillars, which can be traced from the Third Series of printings, shows up more clearly on the chalky paper. The right-hand vertical pillar was broken by the half scoops without dots, and the co-extensive line alongside showed four fine clear cuts, two at the top and two at the bottom of this line. The white dot found in other printings from this plate under the N of PENCE below the sixth stamp in the bottom row of the sheet shows more clearly on the chalky paper than previously.

Plate 5. The marginal state was the same as for the Sixth, Seventh and Eighth Series of printings, the only change being in the paper. Specimens on the chalk-surfaced paper have been recorded with the variety ' no cross on crown '. This is probably due to faulty printing and not to any defect in the plate.

Marginal blocks showing the distinctive characteristics of some of the plates and printings of the Sixpence are scarce, and some very rare.

Chapter Twenty Eight

Edward VII : Sevenpence

THIS stamp introduced a new value in a new design. Value tablets appeared in the upper corners of the stamp, with the King's head in a large oval. The design resembled the stamps of Nyasaland Protectorate and was undoubtedly the most handsome of the Edward issues. The colour was grey. The spaces round the stamps were filled with fine lines cut by the perforations, like the 4d orange. Eight different monocoloured colour trials are known.

The Imprimatur Sheet was registered on April 24, 1910, and the issue to the public made on May 4. The sheet consisted of 240 stamps in two panes of 120 each, with the panes separated by a row of vertical pillars. The thin marginal lines were co-extensive and similar to those of the Fourpence orange. The De La Rue printings were in shades of slate-grey, ranging from dark to pale. They can be distinguished with certainty from the Somerset House stamps by the fact that the perforation was made by horizontal comb, which left single extra perforation holes at the end of each horizontal line in the side margin. These did not appear on the Somerset House sheets, which were perforated by a vertical comb machine. Three plates were used by De La Rue and all of these were handed over to Somerset House. When the De La Rue contract ended at the end of 1910 there was a very large stock of these stamps on hand ; but printings at Somerset House became necessary as follows :

First Series of Somerset House Printings (*August 1, 1912*). This Series of printings was on rough unsurfaced paper. The marginal lines were co-extensive. There was a single cut under the second stamp in the bottom row of the lower pane and fine ' | | ' cuts under & R below the last stamp. The colour was deep slate-grey.

Second Series of Somerset House Printings (shortly after the First Series, which was very limited). The state was exactly

153

the same as for the First Series, but the paper was plate-glazed and the shades paler.   There was a scoop which encroached on the last pillar under the sixth stamp and the first pillar under the seventh stamp in the bottom row of the upper pane.

Third Series of Somerset House Printings (*December 1912*). There was a single cut in the bottom line of the lower pane below the first stamp, and fine ' || ' cuts under RE below the twelfth stamp in the bottom row.   The shades were slate-grey, as before.

Fourth Series of Somerset House Printings (*May 1913*).   Thin ' || ' cuts under the last stamp in the bottom row of the lower pane below &.   There were no other cuts.   The shades were slate-grey, as before.

Chapter Twenty Nine

Edward VII: Ninepence

THIS value again was similar to its Victorian predecessor, except that the small King's head and the Crown were incorporated in the head-plate ; also the sides were altered to accommodate the words POSTAGE & REVENUE, and one instead of three stars appeared above the ornament which replaced the word REVENUE on the Victorian stamp. As in the case of the 4d and 7d, thin lines of shading cut by the perforation separated the stamps from each other and from the marginal lines. The colours of the De La Rue printings on ordinary paper were very deep purple, deep reddish-purple and very pale purple, and bright blue ranging from pale to deep. The full sheet as printed consisted of 160 stamps in eight panes of 20 each in four rows of five. Four of the panes were arranged in a rectangle constituting the upper half of the sheet as printed ; the other four panes similarly made up the lower half sheet. Each pane was separated from the pane alongside it by a number of alternate purple and blue horizontal lined bars. Below each of the upper two panes in each half sheet were two long bars running the length of each pane and the adjoining short bars, one in blue and the other in purple ; there were similar bars above the upper pair of panes in the lower half sheet, which was made up like the upper half. The full sheets of 160 stamps as printed were divided in half horizontally before issue to Post Offices, so that each Post Office sheet comprised four panes. Throughout all the printings of this stamp, both the purple and blue marginal lines round each pane were continuous. As usual, the De La Rue perforations were by means of a horizontal comb machine.

The Imprimatur Sheet was registered on April 5, 1902, and the stamps printed by De La Rue were issued on ordinary paper on April 7. The colours ranged from pale to very deep purple and pale to deep blue. There were only two head-plates, and one duty-plate.   The head-plate used for all the printings on ordinary unsurfaced paper had no distinguishing marks in the purple marginal lines.   Soon after the stamps on chalk-surfaced paper appeared in 1905, for which both head-plates were used, distinguishing plate cuts were made in the purple lines of the N.W. and S.W. corner panes of both half sheets.   Both these head-plates were handed over to Somerset House at the end of the De La Rue contract, together with the only duty-plate.

On June 29, 1905, chalk surfaced paper first appeared.   The colours ranged from pale brownish-purple to deep chocolate purple, and the blue from quite pale to deep and bright blue.

For the Somerset House printings one head-plate only was used throughout, except for one occasion when the other plate was used for a very short time, presumably while the normal one was undergoing repair from damage which it is known to have sustained.

The printings at Somerset House, which were on ordinary unsurfaced paper and perforated by a vertical comb machine, can be differentiated as follows :

First Series of Somerset House Printings (July 24, 1911).   The colours were a distinctive pinkish- or rosy-purple and shades of pale to rather deep dull blue.   There were no date cuts or dots in any of the panes ; but there was a white dot in the vertical line to the left of the first stamp in the top row of the N.E. corner pane of the lower half sheet.   This printing without date cuts, in pinkish-purple, was small and panes and marginal blocks are scarce.

Second Series of Somerset House Printings (September 1911). There were two purple dots in the margin below the fourth stamp in the bottom row of the S.E. corner panes of both half sheets. Until recently it was believed that these dots appeared only in the lower half sheet.   But one of the Editors has a block with the dots below the fourth stamp in the bottom row of the S.E. corner pane from an upper half sheet.   Therefore sometimes, if not always, they appeared in both half sheets.   These dots are in quite different positions, horizontally and vertically, on different sheets, and Mr L'Estrange Ewen suggested that they must have been

struck by hand, which seems curious, though no better explanation has been forthcoming.   The printing was small and this
variety is rare.

The late S. C. Buckley, in his series of articles in the *Philatelic
Record*, stated that this printing was made in November after the
printing with ' || ' cuts which appeared in October 1911.   But
this is clearly not the case.   The printing with purple dots shows
no trace of ' || ' cuts, whereas clear traces of these appear in the
Fourth Series of printings.   For these reasons, and from the fact
that the succeeding printing appeared in October, it can be
deduced that the second printing became available to the public
in September.

Third Series of Somerset House Printings (October 1911).   There
were wide ' || ' cuts under the fourth stamp in the bottom row
of the S.E. corner pane of the upper half sheet and less wide
' || ' cuts under the fourth stamp in the bottom row of the S.E.
corner pane of the lower half sheet.   On some, but not all, of the
sheets there is a large flaw in the vertical purple line to the right
of the last stamp in the bottom row of the S.E. corner pane in
the upper half sheet.   This flaw also appeared in the Second
Series of printings, proving that they were from the same head-
plate.   The flaw was evidently made good during the course of
the Third Series of printings because some, if not most, of the
sheets show no trace of this.   The shades were rather deep purple
and pale to light blue.

Fourth Series of Somerset House Printings (March 1912).
There were fine ' || ' cuts, very slightly to the right of the star
under the King's head, under the last stamp in the bottom row
of the S.E. corner pane of the upper half sheet ;   and rather
broader ' || ' cuts considerably more to the right under the last
stamp in the bottom row of the S.E. corner pane of the lower
half sheet.   The colours were deep purple, dull greyish-purple
and reddish-purple, and bright blue ranging from pale to deep.
A portion of this Series was in fluorescent purple ink.

At an early stage of the Fourth Series of printings serious
damage occurred towards the bottom of the purple line to the

right of the last stamp in the bottom row of the N.W. corner
pane in both half sheets. In the lower half the damage is more
pronounced. The purple line is not only bulged inwards ; in
addition, the whole of the rounded corner is broken off. In the
upper half sheet the purple line is bulged inwards to a lesser
extent than in the lower half and the rounded corner piece is
not broken off. In both cases the damage was soon repaired,
leaving no traces. It was perhaps during these repairs that
the other head-plate was used temporarily, as above mentioned.
Traces of the date cuts from the Third Series are visible in the
Fourth Series.

Fifth Series of Somerset House Printings (January 1913). There
were thin irregular ' | | ' cuts in the purple line, slightly to the left
of the star below the King's head, under the last stamp in the
bottom row of the S.E. corner pane in the upper half sheet, and
similar (but serrated) cuts to the right of the star under the last
stamp in the bottom row of the S.E. corner pane of the lower
half sheet.   As above mentioned, the single plates cuts and white
dots which appeared in the earlier printings were filled up for the
Fifth Series.   The shades ranged from brownish- and reddish-
purple to black-purple, and from deep cold blue to bright blue.
The reddish-purple shades of some of the stamps from the Fourth
and Fifth Series of printings should not be confused with those of
the First Series, which had an unmistakable rose or pinkish tint.
The First and Second Series of printings were small, and large
pieces (complete Post Office sheets, half such sheets or even panes)
including the south-east portions of S.E. corner panes from these
are rare.   To a lesser degree this applies also to the third printing
(October 1911).   The Fourth Series of printings (March 1912)
lasted for five months until the fifth printing appeared in January
1913.   This was required only until June 30, 1913, when the
Georgian stamps appeared.

Chapter Thirty

Edward VII: Tenpence

IN this case again the new stamp resembled its Victorian predecessor, except for the substitution of the King's head, the addition of a Crown and the words POSTAGE & REVENUE appeared below the King's head on the head-plate. The surrounding purple design also was entirely redrawn. The spaces round each stamp were filled with lines of shading, as in the case of the 4d, 7d and 9d. The Imprimatur Sheet was registered on June 28, 1902, and the issue to Post Offices made on July 3. The arrangement of the sheets as printed consisted of a pane of 48 stamps in four rows of twelve at the top; then followed horizontal purple and carmine line-blocks running right across the sheet; below these was a row of vertical pillars; and below these more horizontal line-blocks right across the sheet; then followed another similar pane of 48 stamps. This made up the upper half sheet. Then followed a row of blank paper; and below this two panes with line-blocks and pillars exactly as in the upper half sheet. Although printed in four panes, the sheet was divided horizontally into two halves before issue to Post Offices. There were continuous purple and carmine marginal lines all round the panes; but there were regular breaks in the purple line between the fourth and fifth and between the eighth and ninth vertical rows at the top and bottom of each pane to facilitate division of the pane into three blocks of 16 stamps. The initial De La Rue printings were on ordinary paper in shades of purple and carmine. The usual horizontal comb perforating machine was used. The ' No cross on Crown ' variety is known in this state.

De La Rue made two head-plates, and there was only one duty-plate. They used both head-plates for printings both on ordinary and chalky paper, but only one head-plate was used for the printing in scarlet. Somerset House used only one head-plate —not the one used by De La Rue for the printing in scarlet.

The chalk-surfaced paper appeared on September 6, 1905. The state was unaltered. The earlier printings on chalky paper were in deep to pale shades of purple and cerise. In September 1910 this was changed to shades of dull to deep purple and scarlet.

The issues from Somerset House on ordinary unsurfaced paper, with vertical comb perforation, were as follows :

First Series of Somerset House Printings (October 9, 1911). The state and marginal settings were unchanged, but red dots were added above the last stamp in the top row of the upper pane and below the last stamp in the bottom row of the lower pane in both half sheets ; there were fairly thick ' || ' cuts in the purple line below the eleventh stamp in the bottom row of the lower pane of the upper half sheet, and similar cuts (slightly more to the left) under the eleventh stamp in the bottom row of the lower pane in the lower half sheet ; also an old single De La Rue plate cut under the first stamp in the bottom row of the lower pane in the lower half sheet (which was filled up for the Second Series of printings). The colours were dull purple and bright scarlet. There were also rare shades of scarlet-vermilion and pink, the latter issued about March 1912. All the ink for this Series of printings is fluorescent. The pink shade shows bright golden-rosine under the quartz lamp. The scarlet shades, and the very rare scarlet-vermilion, show orange-vermilion under the lamp.

Second Series of Printings (May 1912). The state of the plate was the same as before, except that the ' || ' cuts under the eleventh stamp in the bottom row of the lower panes of both half sheets were filled up, and fine ' || ' cuts appeared under the twelfth stamp in the bottom row of the lower pane in each half sheet. The cuts in the upper sheet were under the centre of the stamp, and those in the lower half sheet considerably more to the left. The former single cut under the first stamp in the bottom row of the lower pane in the lower half sheet was filled up. The shades of this series of printings were dull to fairly deep purple and carmine. The ink is not fluorescent, but under the lamp both the carmine and purple appear as deep chestnut. At the end of this Series plate-glazed paper was used. The bluish or slate-purple on this paper appears as bluish-violet under the lamp.

Chapter Thirty One

Edward VII : One Shilling

THIS value also was similar to its bi-coloured Victorian pre-decessor, but with the change of head and the addition of a Crown to the head-plate. A chain of white dots was added round the green head circle and the words POSTAGE & REVENUE were reduced in size. The Imprimatur Sheet was registered on February 25, 1902, and the stamps issued on March 24. The sheet as printed consisted of 240 stamps in two panes of 120 each, arranged in ten rows of twelve. The complete sheet was cut in two horizontally before issue to the Post Offices. The first printings were on ordinary unsurfaced paper. The marginal lines (red inside and green outside) were continuous round the panes. Both lines were cut away at the corners of the panes.

De La Rue made two combined head- and duty-plates and three frame plates. Two head- and-duty-plates and two frame plates were used for the printings on ordinary paper. The two head-and-duty plates were used for the printings on chalky paper, with one frame plate as used for the ordinary paper, and another which had not been so used. Somerset House used both the head-and-duty plates, but only one of the frame plates. The colours on ordinary paper were slight shades of deep bright carmine and green varying from palish dull green to olive. The perforation of the De La Rue stamps was by the usual horizontal comb machine, leaving single extra perforation holes at the sides of the sheets.

The chalk-surfaced paper appeared on September 6, 1905. There were two settings—one with both lines broken at the corners, as for the printings on ordinary paper, and the other with the green line only broken, and the red line unbroken, at the corners. The colours on the chalky paper were bright carmine and green ranging from dull greyish to very dark (almost black) green. Specimens on chalky paper with inverted watermark have been recorded.

11   161

The printings from Somerset House all had the same marginal arrangement, i.e. with the red lines continuous all round the panes, including the corners, and the green lines also continuous, but cut away at the corners of the panes, similar to the later De La Rue printings. The perforation was by vertical comb.

The First Series of Somerset House Printings appeared on July 17, 1911. It had no date cuts in the marginal lines of either pane. The green was very deep, almost black, combined with bright scarlet. There were no red dots above or below either pane. This printing in black-green without date cuts is rare.

Second Series of Somerset House Printings (October 9, 1911). The marginal lines were unchanged ; but ' | | ' cuts appeared under the eleventh stamp in the bottom row of both panes. The cuts in the upper pane were $2\frac{3}{4}$ mm wide, and in the lower pane $2\frac{1}{4}$ mm. At first there were no red dots above or below either pane ; but soon a red dot appeared above the last stamp in the top row of both panes and below the last stamp in the bottom row of both panes. The earlier variety without the red dots is scarce. The colours were dark to very dark green and slight shades of scarlet.

Specimens from this series of printings with watermark inverted are well known. It appears that at least five, and possibly six, sheets with this abnormality were printed, portions of which survived in unused condition. Before the First World War, Mr L'Estrange Ewen had an upper pane on which the watermarks were badly misplaced vertically, and portions of two watermarks appeared inverted on each stamp, because the horizontal perforation cut the Crowns of the watermark below the centre. The pane concerned also included two stamps practically without a watermark. Mr Ewen demonstrated how this occurred in the following way. A sheet of watermarked paper was printed upside down. The sheet had, in addition to 240 Crown watermarks, the word POSTAGE in double-lined capitals in the margin at the bottom, and watermarks of horizontal lines which normally appear in the margin under the first two and last two stamps in the bottom row of the lower pane. When the sheet was placed upside down on the plate, the watermark POSTAGE and horizontal lines which would normally have appeared in the bottom margin of the lower pane actually fell, *inverted*, along the top row of stamps in the upper pane. Consequently this top row of stamps was watermarked as follows : (*a*) the first and second, and eleventh and twelfth stamps had as watermark portions of the horizontal lines which normally appeared below the first two and last two stamps in the bottom row of the lower pane ; (*b*) stamps numbered 4 to 9 had as watermarks portions of the word POSTAGE inverted ; and (*c*) *every* stamp in the top row (including of course Nos 3 and 10) showed at the bottom along the frame line a small portion, about 2 mm wide, of the bottom of an inverted Crown. Each stamp in the remaining nine rows had the top of an inverted Crown at the top of the stamp and the bottom of an inverted Crown at the bottom of the stamp. Nothing is known of the other pane of the sheet concerned. Probably it was issued in the normal way without its abnormalities being noticed ; and used copies therefrom may have survived.

Since the discovery of the upper pane referred to above, specimens from at least four, and possibly five, other sheets with inverted watermark have been identified. Two of these have the watermarks even lower in relation to the stamps than the Ewen pane. On these no portions of the Crowns appear on the stamps in the top row of the upper panes, and in consequence stamps Nos 3 and 10 in the top row are completely devoid of any sort of watermark. It would seem that not more than four of such stamps could have existed. Another sheet (and possibly two) shows the Crown watermarks almost exactly bisected by the horizontal perforations ; and on another sheet the horizontal perforations cut the Crowns about one-third of the way down. No information is available to indicate the numbers of the stamps from the various sheets concerned which were saved and became available to collectors, but all these varieties of inverted watermark are of considerable rarity.

11*

Third Series of Somerset House Printings (April 6, 1912). The colour was changed to deep carmine (from scarlet) and shades of deep green. The marginal setting was the same as before, with carmine dots above and below the last stamps in the top and bottom rows of both panes. In the upper pane there were fine ' | | ' cuts in the green line below the middle of the last stamp in the bottom row ; in the lower pane there were similar cuts, but considerably more to the left.

Fourth Series of Somerset House Printings (December 30, 1912). The red dots were removed from above and below the last stamps in the top and bottom rows of both panes. The ' | | ' cuts under the last stamps in the bottom rows of both panes were the same as for the Third Series of printings. A portion of this Series was on highly plate-glazed paper.

Chapter Thirty Two

Edward VII : Two Shillings and Sixpence

THE general design of this value resembled that of its Victorian predecessor, but there were material differences. Apart from the change of head and the addition of a Crown, there were no corner letters, the frame for the head was re-drawn, the value was expressed at the bottom wholly in words, and the stamp was larger. The inscription at the top was POSTAGE & REVENUE, as before. The paper was fiscal paper with watermark large Anchor. The sheet consisted of 112 stamps in two panes, one above the other, each comprising 56 stamps in seven rows of eight. The panes were separated by a row of line-blocks or pillars. The sheets as printed were cut in half before issue to Post Offices ; therefore a Post Office sheet consisted of one pane. Each pane was surrounded by a continuous marginal line which was rounded at the outer corners. As the side marginal lines ran from the upper to the lower pane, enclosing the pillars, the inner corners of the marginal line were square. This state was maintained for all the printings of this value. The perforation was 14 made by a horizontal comb machine for the De La Rue issues. The Imprimatur Sheet was registered on December 27, 1901, and issue to the public made on April 5, 1902.

The first issues printed by De La Rue on unsurfaced paper were in dull purple and lilac shades. It is important to remember that for this value, and all the other high value stamps, the perforation used by De La Rue was a horizontal comb which left an extra perforation hole in every horizontal line of perforation on each side of the sheet ; whereas for the Somerset House printings the perforation was by vertical comb, which left no such extra perforation holes at the sides. With side marginal copies therefore, the distinction between the printings is beyond any doubt. Copies with watermark inverted have been recorded for this value, both on ordinary and on chalk-surfaced paper.

The chalk-surfaced paper appeared on October 7, 1905. The colour consisted of shades of deep purple, reddish purple and lilac. The gum was yellowish and sometimes blotchy. This was the only value above One Shilling which appeared on chalk-surfaced paper. For the Two Shillings and Sixpence, Five Shillings, Ten Shillings and One Pound values only one plate was used by De La Rue for each value, and all these were handed over to Somerset House.

The printings at Somerset House on unsurfaced paper were as follows :

First Series of Somerset House Printings (September 27, 1911). There were purple dots above the last stamp in the top row and below the last stamp in the bottom row of both panes ; and ' | | ' cuts in the marginal line below the penultimate stamp in the bottom row of each pane. The cuts in the upper pane were 1 mm wide, under & ; those in the lower pane were $1\frac{1}{2}$ mm wide under IX. The colour was shades of lilac and pale dull purple, and the ink was fluorescent. The gum was colourless.

Second Series of Somerset House Printings (June 1912). The state was the same as before ; but the ' | | ' cuts now appeared under the last stamp in the bottom row of each pane. The cuts in the upper pane were under the second S of SHILLINGS, and in the lower pane under the G. There were shades of deep purple, black-purple and dull purple. A portion of this Series was on plate-glazed paper.

Third Series of Somerset House Printings (March 18, 1913). The state and date cuts were exactly the same as for the Second Series, but a white dot was added in the vertical marginal line alongside the last stamp in the bottom row of each pane. The colour was shades of reddish-purple, which differed materially from any shade of the previous printings. Most, if not all, of the printings of this Series were on highly plate-glazed paper.

Chapter Thirty Three

Edward VII: Five Shillings

THE inscription at the top of this value was POSTAGE only. There were no corner letters ; and the design and ornamentation differed materially from those of the Victorian stamps. In addition to the change of head, a Crown was added, as usual.

The state and make-up were the same as for the Two Shillings and Sixpence. The same fiscal paper with watermark large Anchor was used. The Imprimatur Sheet was registered on February 13, 1902, and the stamp issued on April 5, 1902. Only ordinary unsurfaced paper was used for this value. The De La Rue perforation 14 was, as usual, by means of a horizontal comb.

The colour of the De La Rue stamps was bright carmine with only slight shades from deep to medium ; but in March 1912 (after the Somerset House printings had begun to appear) specimens were issued at the Holborn Post Office in exceptionally deep shades of carmine on paper with very transparent yellowish gum. The ink of most of the De La Rue stamps shows a vivid blood-red flash-up under the quartz lamp.

The Somerset House printings, with vertical comb perforation, colourless gum and red dots above the last stamp in the top row, and below the last stamp in the bottom row of each pane, were as follows :

First Series of Somerset House Printings (February 29, 1912). There were ' | | ' cuts under the penultimate stamp in the bottom row of each pane. In the upper pane they were very fine, upright, about ½ mm wide, and situate under the first I of SHILLINGS. In the lower pane they were in a similar position, but thicker, slanting slightly to the left and about 1 mm wide.

Second Series of Somerset House Printings (October 1912). This Series was exactly the same as the First, except that the ' | | ' cuts were under the last stamp in the bottom row of each pane.

In the upper pane they were under the first I of SHILLINGS, and about $1\frac{1}{2}$ mm wide.   In the lower pane they were below LL and about $1\frac{1}{4}$ mm wide.

Generally speaking, the colour of the Somerset House printings was slightly paler than the De La Rue stamps, but some of the latter are paler than the normal Somerset House shades.   Apart from the date cuts, the perforation and gum constitute better methods of differentiation between the printings than the colour and execution.   Part of the issue of October 1912 fluoresces with a faint golden emission, indicating a certain eosin content in the ink.

Chapter Thirty Four

Edward VII : Ten Shillings

THIS was an entirely new design. The King's head on shaded background was surrounded by an octagonal frame surmounted by a Crown. The word POSTAGE only appeared at the top and TEN SHILLINGS at the bottom. The value was also expressed in figures on both sides. The rest of the design consisted of elaborate ornamentation. The usual unsurfaced fiscal paper with large Anchor watermark was used, and the perforation of the De La Rue stamps was by horizontal comb. Like the preceding high values, the sheet consisted of 112 stamps in two panes of 56 each in seven rows of eight. The sheet was cut in two horizontally before issue to Post Offices, so that a Post Office sheet was a single pane. Again there were continuous marginal lines round the panes and running from pane to pane. There was the usual row of pillars between the panes. The right-hand vertical marginal line had a cut below the bottom of the last row of stamps in the upper pane, and a similar cut above the top row of stamps in the lower pane. The Imprimatur Sheet was registered on July 25, 1902, and the stamps were issued on August 5. The colour varied from pale to rather deep ultramarine, the latter being the less common.

The Somerset House printings were as follows :

First Series of Somerset House Printings (January 14, 1912). The shades were much the same as the De La Rue stamps, but in general less bright. The perforation was by vertical comb ; the gum was colourless, and small blue dots appeared above the last stamp in the top row and below the last stamp in the bottom row of each pane. The marginal lines were continuous round the panes, as before. Very fine ' | | ' cuts appeared in the marginal line below the upper pane just between the seventh and last stamps, so that when the vertical perforation was centred exactly between these stamps it was liable to bisect the cuts, which then

became almost invisible unless careful inspection is made.   Per-
haps consequently this variety is rare.   The ' | | ' cuts in the lower
pane were thick and under the S.E. corner square of the seventh
stamp in the bottom row.

Second Series of Somerset House Printings (July 24, 1912).
The state was the same as for the First Series, except that the ' | | '
cuts appeared under the last stamp in the bottom row of both
panes.   The cuts in the upper pane were only about $\frac{1}{4}$ mm apart
below LL ;   those in the lower pane were about 1 mm wide, the
right-hand one slanting to the right.

Chapter Thirty Five

Edward VII : One Pound

THIS value had a certain resemblance to its Victorian predecessor, but many differences. The shape was oblong, its horizontal length occupying the space of three normal stamps of the values with Crown watermark, and consequently had three Crowns as watermark. The outer frame resembled the Victorian stamp, but there were no corner letters. In addition to the change of head and incorporation of a Crown, the whole of the centre around the King's head was ornately re-designed. The value appeared in large white symbols and figures on both sides of the head, and in words in a tablet at the bottom. The perforation was by means of a special horizontal comb, leaving an extra perforation hole in the margin on one side of the sheet only, the other side of the sheet being perforated through. Whether the single extra perforation hole appeared on the left or the right of the sheet depended upon whether the sheet was fed into the perforating machine from the top or from the bottom. The sheet consisted of 80 stamps in two panes of 40 each, one above the other, in ten rows of four ; but the sheet was cut up into single panes before issue to the Post Offices. Each pane was surrounded by continuous green lines which, as usual in the monocoloured stamps, ran across from one pane to the other ; and between the panes was the usual row of vertical pillars. These, however, were wider apart than for the other values, there being only eleven pillars above and below each adjoining stamp, though twelve would have been normal, since this stamp was three times as wide as the ordinary stamps with Crown watermark. Ordinary unsurfaced paper only was used.

The Imprimatur Sheet was registered on March 3, 1902, and the issue printed by De La Rue was made on July 16. The colour was bluish-green varying only slightly in shade.

The Somerset House printings which were generally slightly deeper in shade, and not quite so finely executed, were as follows:

First Series of Somerset House Printings (September 3, 1911). There being only four stamps in a row, the ' || ' date cuts appeared in the marginal line under the last stamp in the bottom row of each pane. Those in the upper pane were upright, about $1\frac{1}{2}$ mm wide and just to the right of N in POUND ; those in the lower pane lean to the right and are about $1\frac{1}{2}$ mm wide. They were slightly more to the right than those in the upper pane. The gum was colourless. There were no coloured dots above or below the panes. The perforation was again effected by the special horizontal comb leaving an extra perforation hole on one side of the sheet only.

Second Series of Somerset House Printings (April 1912). The state was the same as for the First Series, except that the ' ll ' cuts were filled up, and instead there appeared a white dot in the marginal line below, and *above* the last stamp in the bottom *and top* rows of both panes. All these dots are situate in line with the right hand side of the value tablet at the bottom of the stamp. The gum was again colourless.

THE LOWDEN FORGERY

There is a well-known forgery of the One Pound stamp known as the ' Lowden forgery '. It is scarce and much more valuable than the genuine stamp. Large numbers were made by photo-lithography from a block of eight genuine stamps. They were stuck on brown paper and cancelled with an obliterator resembling that used in the Channel Islands, where One Pound stamps were largely used for the payment of Customs Duty on parcels of tobacco destined for the United Kingdom. The recipients of the parcels were in the habit of cutting off the used stamps and selling them to dealers, thereby recouping themselves a substantial portion of the duty paid.

A large parcel of stamps purporting to come from this source was bought from Lowden by a stamp dealer for a large sum of money. The sale was effected after dark, when the stamps by artificial light seemed quite genuine. However, when they were inspected by daylight, they did not look so good, and they were all found to be forgeries. Lowden was prosecuted and convicted, and most of the stamps were destroyed, but a certain number survived for dealers and collectors. The paper was of a different texture and rather thinner than the genuine article. The watermarks were roughly impressed and not woven into the texture of the paper ; but the perforation was accurate ; the colour was too pale and yellowish. In the genuine stamp the impression is sharp with a clear background ; the lines of the shading are continuous ; the Crown is complete ; and the shading round the King's head is formed of *white* lines on a *solid* background. The forgery has a blurred impression with an indistinct background ; the lines of shading are faint and broken ; the Crown is imperfect ; and the shading round the King's head is formed of *coloured* lines on a *white* ground. By artificial light a large parcel of these stamps was good enough to extract from a dealer a large sum of money. If he had managed to save more of them from the destruction upon which the Authorities insisted, he might have recovered his money. Besides being interesting forgeries, specimens constitute souvenirs of a philatelic prosecution which caused quite a sensation.

SUMMARY

In studying the Edward VII stamps it is important to remember the following points :—

(*a*) The cuts in the lines of marginal rule which were made in most of the plates by De La Rue only identify and distinguish plates, and do not necessarily give any indication of date of issue of the sheet concerned, since some plates were used over long, and sometimes broken, periods.

(*b*) A few of the plates have no plate cuts ; some which originally had none, had them added later ; and in some cases plate cuts were filled up.

(*c*) When a plate has no De La Rue cut, it can be identified by other means—e.g. continuous or coextensive lines, rounded or square corners at inner corners of panes, lines at sides only or all round panes, corners rounded or cut away, lines distorted, broken, nicked, etc.

(*d*) Certain differences in the state of a plate are due to its having had the steel surface renewed, or to cleaning or repair.

(*e*) The plate cuts are usually located in the bottom marginal line (though sometimes also in the top line, as in the case of the Ninepence) towards the left end, and appear both on head- and duty-plates, as well as on plates of monocoloured stamps.

(*f*) The cuts or dots made at Somerset House indicate the series of printings and the approximate *date* of issue.

(*g*) No date cuts or dots were made by Harrison.

(*h*) Fluorescence, denoting the presence of eosin dye in the ink, can be identified with certainty only by submission to the quartz lamp, and shows as an unmistakable radiance. This must not be confused with what is known as ' flash up ', which is the phenomenon indicated by certain stamps under the lamp, or through the reaction caused by paper which is highly glazed.

Index

Index

Aberystwyth 64

Abnormals 28, 31, 35, 37, 38, 65, 66, 72, 75, 84

America 96

Aniline 119, 127

Avery Collection, The 84

Bacon, Edward 32

Baronet Collection, The 48

Bates, Colonel A. F. 30

Berlin Imperial Postal Museum 4, 6, 23, 25

Bisect 134

Booklets 121, 122, 123, 126, 127

Bradford 59

British Philatelist, The 84, 123

Buckley, S. C. 157

Cancellation, experimental 9

Channel Islands 172

Cheltenham 65

China 93

Colour, changes in 26, 101

Colour trials 23, 26, 80, 94, 96, 101, 102, 106, 107, 110, 111, 112, 125, 128, 132, 135, 140, 153

Constantinople 74

Contract, termination of 117, 156

Crawford Collection, The 21, 28, 30, 35, 46, 65, 74, 129

Crosse and Blackwell 75

Customs and Inland Revenue Act of 1881 94

De La Rue & Co., Thomas 18, 19, 21, 23, 25, 26, 32, 45, 73, 92, 93, 97, 100, 102, 104, 108, 114, 117, 118, 121, 122, 124, 126, 127, 128, 129, 130, 133, 136, 137, 138, 140, 142, 143, 145, 151, 153, 155, 159, 160, 161, 162, 165, 167, 168, 169, 171, 174

Design 25, 94, 98, 114

Dickinson & Son, John 3

Dickinson, paper, details of manufacture 3

Die proofs 75, 76, 82, 90, 100, 115, 133

Dryden Bros. 1

Electrotype process 117

Embossed stamps :
  Condition 10
  Destruction of stamps 15
  Dies, The 11, 15
  Die I 2, 3, 9
  Die II 3, 9, 12

Embossed stamps : (*Contd.*)
  Die III 15
  Die IV 15
  Die, counterpart of 1
  Die, original 2, 7
  Die, primary 1, 2
  Die, proofs 2
  Die, working 2, 7
  Details of sheet 4, 15
  Error, silk thread 11
  Essay, one shilling 9
  Issue, date of 12
  Issue, quantity 12
  Paper 16
  Printings 6
  Quantity printed 14

Envelopes, Mulready 3

Eosin dye 119

Essays 23, 26, 27, 76, 83, 92, 93, 104, 106, 107, 114, 133, 136

Ewen, L'Estrange 156, 162

Expert Committee 60

Ferrary Collection, The 23

Ferté, Jean Ferdinand Joubert de la 18

Flaws 99, 126, 157

Forgery 47, 72, 86, 88, 99, 172

Forgery, Stock Exchange 80

Forme 117

French Government 18

Fuchs, Emil 114, 115, 116, 128, 132, 145

Gibbons Ltd., Stanley 33, 54, 62, 63, 121, 123, 125, 126

Government Printers (*See* Somerset House)

Greenoch 84

Gum 16, 20

Hair lines 61, 71, 72

Halifax 65

Harrison & Sons Ltd. 117, 118, 121, 122, 123, 124, 126, 127, 135, 137, 138, 141, 174

Hill, Ormond 8, 14, 16, 18, 23, 24, 25, 26, 58, 64, 82

Hill, Rowland 12

History of the Stamps of the British Isles 4n, 7, 15, 20n, 36, 40, 45, 47, 53, 54, 59, 60, 63, 64, 65, 66, 69, 71, 72, 73, 74, 79, 83, 85, 86, 88, 91, 95, 104

Holborn Post Office 167

ILLUSTRATIONS

The following illustrations of the various designs issued during the period covered by the text are intended to show the details of the engraving, and have largely been taken from photographs of die proofs or plate proofs printed in black. For the earlier issues this has not always proved practicable, and in some cases early plate proofs in colour have been substituted. The details of the design in the printed stamps are not sharp enough to photograph satisfactorily.

THE EMBOSSED STAMPS

(1847–54)

THE SURFACE PRINTED STAMPS

(1855–56)

(1862)

The Threepence, Fourpence and Ninepence have been reproduced from plate proofs in colour: the Sixpence and One Shilling from die proofs without the corner letters, or plate number of the One Shilling.

THE SURFACE PRINTED STAMPS

(1865)

(1867)

(1872)

THE SURFACE PRINTED STAMPS

(1873)

(1875)

(1876)

(1878)

THE SURFACE PRINTED STAMPS

(1880)

(1881)

(1882)

(1883)

THE SURFACE PRINTED STAMPS

(1883)

(1884)

(1887)

(1890)   (1892)

(1902)

(1910)   (1910)